Crash Course in Marketing for Libraries

Recent Titles in Crash Course Series

Crash Course in Marketing for Libraries

Susan Webreck Alman

Crash Course Series

LIBRARIES
UNLIMITED
A Member of the Greenwood Publishing Group

Westport, Connecticut • London

Library of Congress Cataloging-in-Publication Data

Alman, Susan Webreck.
   Crash course in marketing for libraries / Susan Webreck Alman.
     p. cm. — (Crash course)
   Includes bibliographical references and index.
   ISBN 978-1-59158-430-8 (alk. paper)
   1. Libraries—Marketing. I. Title.
   Z716.3A46 2007
   021.7—dc22   2007013533

British Library Cataloguing in Publication Data is available.

Library of Congress Catalog Card Number: 2007013533
ISBN-13: 978-1-59158-430-8

First published in 2007

Libraries Unlimited, 88 Post Road West, Westport, CT 06881
A Member of the Greenwood Publishing Group, Inc.
www.lu.com

Printed in the United States of America

∞™

The paper used in this book complies with the
Permanent Paper Standard issued by the National
Information Standards Organization (Z39.48–1984).

10   9   8   7   6   5   4   3   2   1

With love and gratitude to Blanche Woolls for all of her support!

Contents

Acknowledgments

With special thanks to the many individuals who provided assistance with the creation of this book:

Elizabeth Koch for the transcription of class presentations

Sara Gillespie for extensive editing, verifying sources, creating examples, and making numerous helpful suggestions

Bonnie McCloskey for researching the final bibliography

Elisa McClain for preparing the John Cotton Dana Materials

Kim Ringler for providing an excellent marketing plan

Leah Rudolph and Gisela Butera for providing marketing materials

Janet Forton for providing marheting material

Blanche Woolls for editing and encouragement

RJ, Jennie, and Christopher for their patience

Introduction

We, librarians, know that libraries provide value to our communities and to society, and for the most part our users recognize the benefits that they receive. Nonusers of libraries rarely argue against the value of libraries, but they often do not recognize or are not aware of the many services that librarians and libraries provide. They need to be made aware, but this task is not solely the responsibility of the library's director.

To the uninitiated, anyone who works in a library is perceived as a "librarian" whether he or she is a custodian, volunteer, or director. Your entire library staff should be coached on how to be library advocates and to market the library to everyone they meet. This guide will help you train your staff to do just that. It offers basic information on how to market libraries to people who work in a library, anyone who uses a library, and perhaps most important, the nonuser of a library's services.

I became involved in marketing a number of years ago and now teach it on a regular basis to graduate students in library and information science. No two marketing courses have been the same, since the students direct the activities based on their areas of interest and expertise. This hands-on course has given people the opportunity to develop marketing plans and projects that have been successfully implemented in libraries. Small projects have developed into major transformations, and students have become change agents for all types of libraries in which they have worked or volunteered. Following are some examples of what students have done after taking my course:

- During a job interview, Mary Evangeliste told her prospective employer that she would really enjoy being involved in marketing. Later her employer agreed to designate part of Mary's time and effort to marketing, although the library had never had a marketing focus. As a result, she formed a marketing committee that comprised a diverse group of people who had different ideas about how to best serve the community. They put together a marketing plan for promoting the library and won a national marketing award for the best campaign. Mary is now the cofounder of Fearless Future, a library marketing consultant firm.

- After the semester-long marketing class and a one-day training session through ACRL's Strategic Marketing for Academic and Research Libraries, Cinda Gibbon became actively involved in marketing in her library. Within a year she was leading a workshop on marketing for other librarians in the region.

- Luke Vilelle was hired to promote the library to the university administration and faculty through public relations efforts and liaison activities.

This book has been developed from the content and activities in my library marketing course. You will acquire the same information that is available in my course from this book. The success of your marketing efforts can be realized if you follow these *Crash Course* guidelines. You are sure to have fun as well as make a difference in your library and the community it serves.

Chapter 1

The Planning Process for Your Marketing Plan

Before you can market your library, you need to create a *marketing plan*. To do so, you must first understand what your library hopes to gain from its marketing campaign. You should also gather information about your community's wants and needs, so that your marketing will be successful. In this chapter I show you how to prepare yourself and your library to create an effective marketing plan.

We start with a quick definition of marketing and then move on to the importance of aligning your marketing plan with your library's strategic plan. You will learn how to collect information about your community and then two ways to analyze your community's needs. Finally, we take a look at the best method(s) to use based on your library's resources.

Remember that just a little knowledge can go a long way in giving you the skills necessary to begin a marketing campaign in your library. But the most important thing you need for marketing is enthusiasm! Many procedures can be followed to develop an effective marketing campaign, but your time and effort will be wasted if your coworkers and volunteers are uninterested. You need to engage your staff and get them involved in the library's activities, and then you will address your community.

Defining Marketing

Before you can begin to market your library, you have to know what marketing means to you. At the beginning of my class I ask students to give me their definitions of marketing. Here are some of the answers I have received:

- A deliberate process for demonstrating one's value or need, which ultimately leads to meeting one's mission (be it through sales, increased use, etc.) (Juliet Greenberg)

- The process of informing and educating a population about a product or service in a way that uses information known about the targeted population, and determining what products or services would benefit them (Lia Thomas)

- Knowing your customers' needs, perspectives, and psychology so that you can effectively convince them how much they need your product or service. Then, making a bridge between the product and the users, effectively communicating to the users exactly why the product is essential or "hot" for them, through advertising, outreach, etc. (Claire Scott)

As you can see, marketing involves understanding what a customer needs, creating a product that will appeal to that customer, and then effectively educating the customer about that product. Marketing libraries is no different. To effectively market your library, you must determine what your community wants, create services that meet their needs, and then educate the community about those services.

The Marketing Planning Process

The plan that you will develop to market your library's services should match the goals and objectives of your library's strategic plan. If your library already has a strategic plan, you should use it to guide your vision of what products and services you want to develop and how you'll market them to the community. For instance, if one of the goals and objectives of your library's strategic plan is to reach preschool children and their caregivers, your marketing plan should target this audience. That way, your marketing plan will fit in with your strategic plan.

What if your library doesn't have a strategic plan? Many libraries don't, but this shouldn't keep them from creating a marketing plan. If your library doesn't have a strategic plan, the first step in planning your marketing campaign is to create a clear vision of what it is you want to accomplish by marketing your library and its services. This clear vision can be articulated in the form of goals and objectives for the project. Simply stated, a "goal" is a statement about what you want to accomplish, and "objectives" are statements that identify how you are going to achieve that goal. If you clearly state your goals and objectives, everyone in your library will know exactly what to work toward.

In either case, the marketing plan cannot be developed until you have a solid understanding of your community. Often librarians have a great marketing idea, and they expend a lot of time and energy developing it without ever considering whether the project or program is relevant to their community. It isn't until the anticipated result hasn't been realized (attendance was poor or circulation was not increased) that people recognize that they should have consulted the intended audience in the first place. It's easy to get caught up in the excitement of an idea and forget this first step, even though it seems obvious that determining what the community wants is critical. An example of this miscalculation was a program planned in Miami, Florida.

Some years ago, a library was being set up north of Miami in a community that has a large Cuban population. The library was in a fabulous location, a storefront right in the heart of the community. The library hired a bilingual librarian especially to work with children, installed an online public access catalog (OPAC), ordered bilingual materials, and put out bilingual posters. The staff were very excited to have this new library in the community, but when they opened their doors, nobody came. They couldn't figure out what they had done wrong. Finally, they talked to a local Cuban man who was well known and well respected in the community and asked, "Can you tell us what we're doing wrong?" He answered, "Well, you've got a computer in your library. Nobody will come to use that. They think that their information will go back somehow and affect their families that are still in Cuba." Once the library staff knew what the problem was, they were able to put out information explaining OPAC and assure the community that their information would not be shared. If the librarians had only asked their potential audience about their concerns and needs, they would have avoided a waste of time and unnecessary expense.

Gathering Data about Your Community

The first step in figuring out how to promote your library to the community is to gather information about that community. This section reviews useful methods that can be used to collect this information: surveys, observation, focus groups, and the nominal group technique.

Surveys

Surveys can be a very valuable means of gathering information about your community's needs, but it's important that you determine exactly what information you want before you write and then conduct a survey. Survey construction is critical to the effective collection of relevant information, so take the time to create questions that will give you the answers you need. Remember that people are very busy, and trying to get them to complete a survey is a challenge. You want to have a survey that is clear and concise and collects the exact information desired. Recently I received a survey that asked about my individual preferences for continuing education coursework but didn't ask for my preferences on how the courses should be delivered (in-person/online or synchronous/asynchronous), the length of courses, the cost of courses, or graduate credit/noncredit. The survey probably would have been much more useful to its authors if it had asked about these preferences.

The first step in creating an effective survey is to make a list of all the kinds of information that are needed. Writing the questions takes practice, so test out your survey on some library users, staff, or neighbors before sending it out. Following are some additional hints on constructing a survey:

- Determine whether another librarian has used a survey to gather information about a similar topic and ask if you can borrow it. Also review the literature. Many articles may be in the "how we did it well" category, but the authors are often willing to share everything about their study. If you called and said, "Do you mind if

I use your survey? Do you mind if I use this idea?" many librarians would give you all kinds of helpful hints. That's the kind of profession we're in!

- Make the survey as clear and concise as possible. People will be more inclined to answer a survey if it takes five minutes or less.

- Surveys should include questions that will elicit the types of responses that are needed.

- Questions should be

    – relevant to the topic,

    – forced choice (providing lots of options),

    – clearly stated,

    – unbiased,

    – written at a sixth-grade reading level, and

    – focused on one topic (not combining two questions into one).

- Reward the people who respond (with a coupon to a local store, waiver of a book fine, a candy bar, etc.).

Once you have chosen the questions you wish to have answered, decide what kind of survey you will conduct, oral or print. If you would like to do an oral survey, you must decide whether to call potential respondents or survey them in person. If you think that it will be better for you to do a print survey, you must decide whether you want to mail the survey, present it in person, or offer it online.

Each of these methods has its benefits and drawbacks. For instance, online surveys can be distributed quickly, but only if you have the correct e-mail addresses for the potential respondents. On the plus side, you will save the costs of printing and mailing the survey. In a print survey, the average rate of return is less than 70 percent and often lower than 40 percent. This means you might not be getting a representative cross-section of the population.

Table 1.1 (p. 6) shows the advantages and disadvantages of each method.

Table 1.1. Advantages and Disadvantages of Survey Methods

	ORAL		PRINT		
	Phone	*In-person*	*Mail*	*In-person*	*Online*
Advantages	Immediate response	Immediate response		Immediate response	
	Respondents can be selected		Respondents can be selected		Respondents can be selected
			Potential to reach a wide range of respondents		Potential to reach a wide range of respondents
Disadvantages	$–$$$ Telemarketing charges—Volunteers or paid staff	$–$$$ Telemarketing charges—Volunteers or paid staff	$$$ Printing and mailing		E-mail addresses change often
		Respondents are random	Delayed response	Respondents are random	Delayed response
		High rate of return	Low rate of return	High rate of return	
Considerations	Time-consuming Potential annoyance	Time-consuming Potential annoyance	Respondent's ability to read	Respondent's ability to read	Respondent's ability to read

There are additional considerations:

- Paper surveys have to be printed and require either oral or written responses.

- Mailed surveys must include return postage to increase the rate of return.

- Distributing paper surveys in the library will probably result in a higher rate of return, but you only get people who already use the library.

- To get responses from nonusers, you must identify the audience and how you will reach them.

Observation

If you want to know whether something is being used in your library, just look around. One of my favorite unobtrusive measures of observation was a library exhibit with a glass case. At the end of every day the librarians would note how many fingerprints or nose prints were on the case to see if people had been engaged with the exhibit. If no fingerprints were observed, the librarians knew that this exhibit did not appeal to the library's users. They could then rethink what kind of exhibits would attract both users and nonusers to the library.

Of course, there are many different ways to do this kind of observation in your library. For instance, before you reshelve items, do counts to see what kind of materials patrons are looking at. If books on one topic or of one genre seem popular, you may want to add more of these books to your collection. Take time to think about what you can observe in your library that will provide clues about the programs and services your patrons desire.

Focus Groups

Focus groups are a useful way to collect information, but they are more costly than surveys and observation because of the time needed to select and interview the groups. It is important that you take the time to preselect the audience and gather a group that is representative of the population you have targeted in your strategic or marketing plan. For instance, if your marketing focus is on teens, you should gather a group of teens who represent a cross-section of the entire community. The library staff should know the community pretty well and be able to identify key people who should be part of your focus group. Once you know whom you'd like to have in your focus group, prepare a special invitation to get the participants to the meeting. It's important for people to feel that you especially want their opinions on the topic. Otherwise they may not come.

When the Carnegie Library of Pittsburgh was undergoing major changes in services and the way it looked, the staff set up focus groups all over the city and spoke to their users and potential users: mothers, professional workers, business members and business owners, and a variety of people from teens through seniors. Although they had many focus groups over a period of time, they always had a facilitator to ask the same questions and a method for recording answers for each focus group.

Additional costs may be associated with focus groups beyond the staff time it takes to conduct them. For instance, most focus group discussions are recorded and transcribed, so you will need to consider transcription costs for the focus groups you conduct. Also, you may need to provide refreshments during the group meetings. Be sure to factor in all these costs when deciding whether to use a focus group to gather information about your community.

Nominal Group Technique

Nominal group technique (NGT) is a nonthreatening method used to collect responses from each person in a group setting. There are variations in how this process is used, and explanations of setting up a NGT session are readily available on the Internet. The goal of NGT is to provide a setting for each individual to contribute his or her ideas one at a time and to have a group discussion after all the ideas have been generated. I like to use NGT because it is a way for everyone to participate without fear of anyone laughing at someone's ideas. Each idea is considered for its merit, and each individual in the group votes anonymously for the top choices. The final vote cannot be contested because the ballots are available for everyone to see.

NGT can be used in groups of about ten to twelve people to generate ideas for a long-range plan or a short-term project. Before the session begins, the facilitator distributes the objective of the discussion and asks the participants to prepare a list of ideas. At the beginning of the session the facilitator allows additional time for each person in the group to write his or her ideas on paper before sharing them with the group.

The facilitator writes each individual's idea on a board or on a flipchart so that everyone in the group can see it. Each person shares one idea per round, and the facilitator continues the rounds until all the ideas have been generated. Each idea is explained by someone who did *not* make the original suggestion, so that "shy" contributors will not be expected to defend their contribution and "boisterous" contributors will not get the floor to promote their ideas.

Each individual selects the five suggestions that he or she likes best and writes them on either an index card or a Post-it™ note. The individual ranks the five suggestions and places the ranked order on the card, 5 being the highest score and 1 being the lowest. Either the anonymous Post-it™ ballots are "stuck" beside the corresponding idea on the flipchart or board, or the index cards are collected and tallied. Those suggestions with the highest scores are then acted upon by the group.

For more information on using NGT, see Appendixes A and H.

Analyzing Your Community's Needs

Now that you have gathered information about your community, it's critical that you develop a structured way to consider all the different circumstances or situations that will have an effect on your library. Working in a vacuum without knowledge of what is important to your community can be an expensive mistake if the library program or service is not ultimately used by the community. A variety of assessment methods can be used to determine the external and internal factors that can affect the use of your library. This chapter discusses two of the most helpful: the environmental scan and SWOT analysis.

Environmental Scan

A number of interchangeable terms are used to define the process of examining the various factors that may have an impact on the library and the community. You may be familiar with terms such as *community analysis, needs assessment,* and *user analysis;* I prefer to use the term *environmental scan*, because it is a more accurate description of the data collection analysis that provides the information you need to make strategic decisions.

An environmental scan is done for each library to determine what factors and issues are affecting that library or the marketing project. You don't want to work in a vacuum, so you will look at all the different circumstances that will have an impact on your library. By doing so, you can get information about your location, your target market, and your community.

For instance, if your target market is preschool children and their caregivers, what kinds of things do you think will affect this population? What would make them want to use the library or not want to use the library? To answer these questions, you should use a combination of the data collection methods listed in the previous section: surveys, observation, and focus groups. You could also look at census data to give you a clear picture of who is in your community and what trends you may be able to expect.

To see an example of a massive environmental scan, take a look at OCLC's *Perceptions of Libraries and Information Resources: A Report to the OCLC Membership*. This scan was conducted by OCLC in 2003 and 2005 and was focused, costly, and comprehensive in scope. Although it's unlikely that you'll ever do an environmental scan on this level, it will give you a good idea of the kind of information you can collect by performing one. Because OCLC gathered data about many types of libraries, you also may be able to use data from these studies to extract information that pertains to your situation. By engaging in an environmental analysis, you can get a very clear picture of your target market and the things your library needs to do to attract this market.

SWOT Analysis

As organizations prepare to develop strategic plans, they often engage in a SWOT (Strengths, Weaknesses, Opportunities, Threats) analysis, which is simply a tool that can be used to assess the internal and external factors affecting the environment. These analyses can be elaborate studies that examine a range of activities, from an analysis of the gross revenue of regional businesses to the preferences of a certain segment of the population, or they may be general overviews of the community and the organization. As you can imagine, this type of analysis also can be used to develop your library's marketing plan.

How do you assess each of the SWOT factors? A SWOT analysis may be conducted by means of

> an informal brainstorming session of staff members,
>
> focus groups,
>
> formal study by an appointed task force or committee,
>
> surveys,
>
> census data,
>
> talking to users, or
>
> reading the local newspaper.

Let's begin by addressing each component individually.

When considering library *Strengths,* make sure you consider both external and internal ones, which might include the following:

- Internal:

  - Knowledgeable, friendly staff

  - Newer staff with fresh ideas

  - One of best collections in specific area

    – Location in relation to community served:

        In heart of city

        Lots of free parking in center of community

        Close to other governmental agencies

- External:

    – Other reasons for people to come to that area:

        Restaurants, shops, other sites that potential users visit

    – Library is main source for information:

        No bookstores in area

Next you need to identify the *Weaknesses* of the library, staff, and community. Following are some examples of potential internal and external weaknesses:

- Internal:

    – Collection not up-to-date due to budget cuts

    – Understaffed

    – Newer staff don't know users or collection

- External:

    – Library is off beaten path and difficult to get to by public transportation

    – Parking not available

    – Hours not convenient

    – Community population decreasing

    – Competition increasing:

        Users finding new ways to access information through bookstores or surfing the Web

    – Difficult to recruit staff or volunteers to area or institution

It is important to recognize that not all strengths are completely positive, nor are all weaknesses necessarily detrimental to the library. Sometimes you need to make lemonade out of the lemons. Just as there are many recipes for lemonade, you will find there are many ways to develop an effective marketing plan, based on both the strengths and the weaknesses of your library.

Once you have identified your library's strengths and weaknesses, determine how they will affect your marketing plan. Weigh the pros and cons of each item as you begin the planning process. Each situation must be analyzed, so determine where attention should be focused.

Example: Library X has a staff that is composed of recent hires.

Strength	Weakness
New ideas	Unfamiliar with collection
New skills	Unfamiliar with community
Change agents	May change too rapidly

On the one hand, having newer staff could be viewed as a strength because there are new people with new ideas and skill sets who are ready to make changes. This same situation could also be viewed as a weakness because newer staff might not be as familiar with the collection or with the people in that community, and too many changes might have an adverse effect on users.

It may help to identify the cause of each weakness through the use of an environmental scan. Look beyond specific library factors to other factors that affect the business of the library. For instance, the reasons why the library's budget was cut could include the following:

- Businesses have left, so the tax base is not as great as it had been.

- People are visiting the new super bookstores rather than coming to the library.

- Users don't know that they can borrow DVDs from the library.

- Users are not aware that the library can obtain books for them even if those books are not in the library's catalog.

Now let's take a look at *Opportunities*. Opportunities may not always be readily apparent, so you need to be creative in your assessment of the situation.

Example: Library X has a staff that is composed of many recent hires.

Strength	Weakness	Opportunity
New ideas and skills	Unfamiliar with collection and community	Begin mentoring new staff to develop collection, programs, and services and introduce them to local constituencies
Change agents	May change too rapidly	Host all-staff and volunteer retreat to begin strategic plan assessment

As another example, your library could have an opportunity to overcome a weakness such as lack of community use by informing the community of library services, programs, and collections. The marketing plan will then include ways in which the community will be informed about library activities.

Let's look at one more example of opportunities. A library that experienced a disaster that destroyed much of its collection and displaced staff from their offices could identify the following internal and external opportunities:

- Internal:

  - Assess needs of users to assist with collection replacement and development

  - Strengthen communication channels within organization

- External:

  - Work with outside partners in community to plan for improvements in collection and building

  - Develop grant proposals to improve collection and building

Now that you've thought about the strengths, weaknesses, and opportunities in your library, it's time to address *Threats*. These are impediments to the programs and services of the library. They focus on an area of library service and the environmental factors that affect that area. Following are examples of threats:

- A public library's video collection could be threatened by the increased use of a new video store in the area or availability of a cable service.

- Library usage can be threatened by the increased use of information technology or the Internet. Users may think, "I can get whatever I need through Google." You can turn this potential threat into an opportunity by promoting the value-added services that are available in your library.

Example: Library X has a staff that is composed of many recent hires.

Strength	Weakness	Opportunity	Threat
New ideas and skills	Unfamiliar with collection and community	Begin mentoring new staff to develop collection, programs, and services and introduce them to local constituencies	Resentment among new staff and continuing staff members
		Begin to record library's history through policies and procedures or an oral history	Organization's "memory" may be lost
Change agents	May change too rapidly	Host all-staff and volunteer retreat to begin strategic plan assessment	Senior staff may be overruled

The SWOT analysis is an especially useful tool for libraries. However, you need to decide which types of data collection method and analysis are best suited for your particular situation. The next section discusses how to ascertain which tools will make the best use of your library's resources, so that you can successfully analyze your community's needs and develop an appropriate marketing plan.

Deciding What Method(s) to Use

The data collection method and analysis you choose are based on the information you need to get from the library's users or nonusers. They also depend on the amount of time and the resources available to you. Starting questions to gather the information you need about the community so that you can develop a strong marketing plan might be,

"How long will it take to collect the data, and how much time and money do I have to analyze those data?" Following are possible answers:

- Lots of time and money to get all of the answers.

- Some time and some money to get answers.

- Are you kidding?! I needed this last week and there is no money.

Your data collection will be driven by how you answer those questions. Let's take a closer look at the possible responses.

Lots of Time and Money

Although the last answer is a common response from most librarians, we'll start with the first one. Let's suppose you have lots of time and lots of money available. With lots of money, you can hire a consulting firm or bring in a consultant to assess the library and the community of users and nonusers. Consultants develop assessment tools, gather and analyze data, and report the results. If you don't know how to find a consultant, you might find a local educational institution whose faculty and students will create and conduct your survey. You could participate in studies such as LibQUAL, a proprietary service from the Association of Research Libraries, which provides librarians with ways to assess their services as they prepare for planning and marketing.

Consultants or consulting agencies are a luxury that can be used in some library situations. When information derived from data collection and analysis is a high priority for the planning process, funds may be available. If you are able to hire a consultant, you will need to understand the variety of survey methods available. For more information about survey methods, see the "Gathering Data About Your Community" section of this chapter.

It's likely, however, that you won't be able to hire a consultant to perform your data collection and analysis for you. Let's look at some other alternatives, if you have some time and some money.

Some Time and Some Money

"Some time and some money" is a very realistic response for many librarians. Following are some suggested procedures for librarians who have some lead time and a budget allocation, even if it is just a small amount of money:

- Search the literature for surveys that address the issues of concern to you.

- Assess the pros and cons of the different survey formats in regard to time and costs for data collection and analysis:

  – oral—by telephone or in person

  – print—by mail, in the library, or off-site

  – electronic

- Conduct the survey and prepare for data analysis prior to completion. Then assess the information derived from the survey and make an informed decision.

- Set up focus groups.

With these resources you have some flexibility. Choose the method that fits your time and budget allocation and make it work for you!

No Time and No Money

Librarians who are in a hurry and have no budget might try the following:

- Implement the nominal group technique (NGT) with staff and volunteers.

- Use the NGT with a local group of library users or nonusers.

  – Librarians should be connected to the community at large through membership in associations or committees.

- Do a literature review to determine if needed information exists.

  – Networking: Call colleagues in similar libraries to ask about their experiences.

  – Meet with established Friends of the Library groups (see chapter 4 for details) to seek their advice.

– Check studies that contain data relevant to your needs. Potential sources include

> census data to understand demographic changes in the community,
>
> studies conducted in the community, and
>
> national studies such as the OCLC Environmental Scan.

- Study in-house statistics for circulation and door counts for regular service or events.

You can use any combination of the data collection and analysis methods described in this chapter to determine which library services best meet your community's needs. Be creative! The goal is to get the information needed to create an effective marketing plan.

Putting It All Together

If public librarians are interested in promoting resources and services to their clientele, they might ask the community the following questions:

- What kinds of things do you think will affect library usage?

- Why would you want or not want to use the library?

Following are possible responses that could affect your library use:

- They need to use the library for research or study.

- They use the library computers for online searches.

- They don't know how to use reference resources; the library intimidates them.

- Music, food, and drink are not allowed in the library.

- The hours are convenient/inconvenient.

- The location is convenient/inconvenient.

- The furniture is comfortable/uncomfortable

- The librarians are helpful/unhelpful.

- The librarians are friendly/unfriendly.

- Resources are available/unavailable.

- The library is attractive/unattractive.

Using this list of items important to library patrons, you can assess the internal strengths of the library. You could conclude that the library has a pleasant atmosphere, comfortable chairs, plenty of workstations, and extensive hours; is accessible to the community; and has excellent print and electronic resources, including a great selection of full-text databases. A SWOT analysis might indicate that in spite of these strengths, the library has significant weaknesses: under-utilization and patron dissatisfaction.

The next step for the librarian is to decide how to utilize these strengths and weaknesses to optimize new marketing opportunities to prevent the threat of potential budget cuts due to under-usage. Before you can plan a course of action, you need to find information about your users. You can't just assume that you know what they are thinking. Sometimes you can guess correctly, but there's no sense wasting time and money on your marketing activities unless you have some concrete data to ensure that you will achieve the desired results.

Following are some ways to use planning techniques to handle this situation and to market the library:

- Develop a focus group composed of patrons to determine which of the following is the best way to reach them and promote the library's resources:

    - Web site

    - brochure

    - e-mail

    - newspaper ads

    - posters

    - raffle or giveaway (T-shirts, flash drives, etc.)

- Develop a survey to determine

    - why patrons use or do not use the library and

    - whether patrons know about the resources available to them.

- Promote the electronic databases, AND how they can be used by patrons, AND how to use them.

The next chapter discusses how to create a marketing plan. It also covers how to evaluate marketing projects. If you're going to spend time, money, and effort creating and implementing a marketing plan, you want to know whether you've done a good job, so that you can emulate the plan the next time around or make changes if it wasn't so successful.

The rest of the book discusses public relations, working with the press, and how to use different media to appeal to various groups. Fund-raising and development are also covered, because they have become more of a necessity in all types of libraries and also fall under the topic of marketing. There's certainly much to learn about marketing, but let's take it one step at a time! In chapter 2 we begin the marketing plan.

Chapter 2

Develop a Marketing Plan

After completing the planning process, it's time to develop your marketing plan. You can think of the marketing plan as a map: You've decided what your goal should be (what services and programs your library would like to market), and now it's time to figure out how to get there. Your marketing plan will outline the best and most efficient way of reaching that goal.

The marketing plan is an organizational tool. It allows you to make targeted decisions about your marketing ideas and then helps you organize and implement these ideas. It also makes the entire staff aware of the library's marketing goals and the process to follow to reach them.

The last chapter presented a library that would like to increase the number of preschool children and their caregivers who come into the library. Since this goal was in line with the library's strategic plan, the library staff researched the community and then came up with ideas for ways to market the library's services, collection, and programming to this group of people. These marketing ideas will be the foundation for the library's marketing plan. The plan itself will lay out the process of implementing these strategies to get to the end result: raising awareness about library services and attracting preschool children and their caregivers to the library.

This chapter introduces the basic components of a marketing plan. It takes an in-depth look at each of these components so that you can create a marketing plan for your own library, followed by examples of marketing plans that have been constructed by various libraries. It's important to look at marketing plans from many sources, since there are many formats for these plans. You can decide which format works best for you and your library.

Marketing Plan Components

Although marketing plans can follow various formats, almost all plans include the following components:

> an executive summary,
>
> an environmental scan,
>
> marketing goals and objectives,
>
> a marketing plan or strategy,
>
> an action plan,
>
> a budget, and
>
> an evaluation.

Let's take a look at each of these components.

The Executive Summary

The executive summary is the global overview of everything that will be presented in the marketing plan. It can be used for two purposes:

- as an introduction to the marketing plan itself, or

- as an overview of the marketing plan to be presented for funding or approval from another authority.

Although the executive summary appears first in the marketing plan, it will actually be written last, since it is a reflection of everything that occurs in the plan. As you read the description of the marketing plan, don't worry if you're not sure exactly what to include. It should become apparent after you create the rest of your plan.

Introduction to Your Organization

At the beginning of the executive summary, you should introduce your organization, especially if the summary will be read by someone outside the library. Give highlights of your library. For example, if your library has an interesting history, include information about it. You might also want to talk about the strengths of your collection, staff, programs, and services. Think about the SWOT analysis discussed in chapter 1. What strengths did you determine were a part of your library? Include those in the executive summary, if they're relevant.

If you already have a boilerplate that you use for library marketing materials, you can use it in the executive summary. A *boilerplate* is a standard—and brief—description of your library that can be used for a number of different purposes. It gathers statistics about your library (usage, strengths of the collection, etc.) and explains the importance and relevance of the library, the collection, and the staff. If you don't already have a boilerplate, you should create one and keep it up to date. (An example is provided in Appendix B.) You will use the information in your boilerplate to write a grant proposal or an executive summary. You have ready access to the facts you need.

While we're on the subject, you should also prepare an "elevator speech" about your library to have on hand when the need arises. Let's say you're in an elevator and the president of a company that you would like to get funding from happens to be in the elevator with you. Are you going to stand there and look at the floor that whole time, or are you going to make your point because you have that person as a captive audience? You want to market your library! If you have memorized the relevant points that you want to say, you can be ready in a minute to give your speech. Just give the highlights and any relevant statistics. Here's an example: "I'd like to take this opportunity to tell you about an exciting project that we're trying to get underway at the library. And did you know our library serves 500 children and their parents?" Prepare what you'd want to say to people if you had their attention for two minutes, the time it takes to go up in an elevator. And then have extra things to say in case the elevator gets stuck! Some of the statements you use in your elevator speech can also be used in your executive summary.

Mission Statement and Goals and Objectives

In your executive summary you may also include your library's mission statement and its goals and objectives. These may be imported from the strategic plan, if your library has one. If it doesn't, don't worry. Just think about your library's goals and list them clearly. Remember that your marketing plan should be aligned with the library's broader goals, so you've probably already outlined these objectives for yourself. Include them, in a clear and concise way, in the executive summary.

List of the People Involved in the Marketing Plan

Your executive summary should also include a list of those who are going to be involved in the marketing project. You don't have to list every person who works in the library, but you should highlight the key players. For instance, if your marketing plan is aimed at bringing preschool children to the library, you would say in the executive summary that the youth or children's librarian will be a part of the project. You should identify any others in the cast of characters and, if you think it's necessary, briefly explain the structure of your organization. Explain the major points of your plan, although not in detail, since the detail comes later in the plan.

Summary of the Marketing Objectives and Recommended Strategies

The executive summary is a power-packed statement that identifies your marketing need. It should be no more than two pages long and, with careful writing, you can get it down to one page. Remember that it's an overview. Since you may be giving it out to a number of different people, you don't want it bogged down with extraneous information. Again, the executive summary comes first, but it isn't written until the very end.

The Environmental Scan

In this section you should outline the results of the environmental scan (discussed in chapter 1). This section does not have to be long; just provide information about your location, your target market, and the competitive environment. Also, you should identify any key issues that your organization faces.

Marketing Goals and Objectives

In this section you should state your marketing goals and objectives, which are an essential part of your marketing plan. If you think of your marketing plan as a map for a successful marketing campaign, the goal is the destination and the objectives are the landmarks along the way. You're not going to vary from the route that you've set up.

The marketing goal, then, is the major thing you want to accomplish in your marketing campaign, such as increasing awareness of your product among your target audience. It could be one thing or more than one. The marketing objectives follow the goal; these are the steps you will follow to reach the goal and complete the marketing plan. They are also what you use to measure whether you have reached your goal.

In our example, the library's goal is to get more parents and caregivers to know about the library's programs, resources, and collections for preschool children. The objectives for the library might be to increase story hour attendance and increase circulation of preschool-age materials.

You should also include in this section the time frame for achieving your marketing objectives. That way, you'll have a path to follow when using your marketing plan.

The Marketing Plan and Strategy

The strategy is your game plan for achieving your marketing objectives. It is essentially the heart of your marketing plan and covers the four "Ps" of marketing:

> **P**roduct
>
> **P**rice
>
> **P**romotion
>
> **P**lace

This method has been developed for the profit sector, but you can modify it for your library.

Let's take a look at the first "P": *product.* Describe your library's product or service in detail. Don't forget to include its features and benefits. Just because you're not actually selling something doesn't mean that you don't have anything to offer your community. Perhaps you are implementing a new service or building a new collection. Or maybe you now have many more board books for babies in your collection, which should appeal to new parents.

The second "P" is *price.* How much will this service or product cost, and how will it be funded? The service probably won't cost your user anything, but it will cost you and your library time and effort. You must ask yourself if you will incur some real costs associated with your production, perhaps a mailing. You also have to figure out how much staff time the service will take, since this is also a real cost. When we discuss the budget later in this chapter, you'll have a better idea of the costs of your marketing project. Since budgets are tight in so many institutions, you'll need to think about how your plan will be funded. Will the money come from your regular budget, or are you going to ask somebody for money for this project?

Now let's talk about the third "P": *promotion.* Describe the promotional tools or tactics you'll use to accomplish your marketing objectives. This is an especially important part of the market plan, because even if you have a fabulous program, no one will come if they don't know about it. In this section you should cover how you're going to promote your product or service. Remember that an important part of promotion is making clear to potential users how your program will benefit them. If you're trying to get preschool children and their caregivers into your library, you need to make it clear to the caregivers that your program will benefit their children.

Place is the fourth "P." Most likely your marketing program will occur in your library. But perhaps there's a better place to host your event, like outside or at a community center. Think about what will be the best place for users to access your service. If the product will be held in the library, where will you hold it? If it's a display, will you display it in a glass case?

The Action Plan

The action plan section is your marketing "to do" list. It includes an outline of specific tasks and describes what will be done, when each task will begin or be completed, who will accomplish the tasks, and the resources assigned to the project. This is one of the most important sections of the plan, and it needs to be thought out in advance, although many librarians don't do so. However, doing this will save a lot of time and trouble later and will help you avoid any unpleasant surprises. You don't want to find out too late that you hadn't considered everything and the costs have become prohibitive.

Although this sounds like what is more formally called "project management," it isn't that elaborate. Just look at what needs to be accomplished and think about the best way to do it. For example, if you were going to hold an early childhood program, you may want to hold the event before the library opens so that the librarian is not distracted by other patrons needing help.

Think about every aspect of the program, including the work before the event and after it. Figure out how to promote your service or product: Who's going to write the press release? Who's going to identify the media? Who's going to be available to do an interview, should it be needed? Also, who's going to develop the invitations, and how will they be sent? The other thing to think about is how to capture the event for later records. Will someone take pictures or record it? Make sure that your program is captured on film so that the pictures can go in your newsletter or your annual report.

The Budget

In this section, list the cost of the marketing activities you are describing in the rest of the marketing plan. Your obvious costs are staff time, printing, and publication costs, but there may be hidden costs as well.

You should pay attention to staff costs, because if a staff member is in charge of the program, that person may not be able to perform his or her regular duties. Will you have to bring in somebody else to run the program or help in the library? What are the real costs associated with this? If it's going to take someone fifty hours to do the program, how much would fifty hours' worth of salary and benefits be?

You're also most likely going to have to print up things like promotional materials and handouts. Even if you're doing the printing in-house, there's a cost associated with the paper and the photocopying. If you decide to set up a Web site, that's going to cost in terms of people who will do it, unless you have volunteers. However, even using volunteers has a certain cost because someone at your library will have to oversee their instruction and engage in a certain amount of monitoring their progress.

If you've ever written a grant proposal for funds, you may begin to see that there is not much difference between that and a marketing plan. Many of the components are similar. If you have the basic skills for strategic planning and writing a grant, you have a head start on preparing a marketing plan. These skills come into play over and over again in a library. If you learned strategic planning and how to write a grant proposal, you can certainly draw on that experience when thinking about the budget for your marketing project.

The Evaluation

An important part of the marketing plan is the evaluation section. Evaluation is built into the marketing plan at the beginning and should be decided on before, not after, the program begins. You need to set up in advance your measures for success. They're really nobody else's measures but your own, but you want to know if you have reached your target goal, fallen short, or exceeded it. For every part of your plan, you should set up some measure by which to evaluate it. A measure may simply be comparing the number of people you would like to attend the program to the number who actually do, or it could be the number of articles about the program that appear in the newspaper, on the radio, or in other media. Following are some other ideas for how to measure and evaluate your program:

Use circulation statistics.

Count the amount of money raised.

Count the number of people getting new library cards.

Do door counts.

Count the number of Web site hits.

Count the number of items (like coffee mugs) purchased.

Do a survey of people who attended the program.

Remember that it's okay if you fall short of your goal; you can always learn from your mistakes. It's better to have a measure and realize that you didn't meet it, rather than saying, "Oh this was a great success" when it truly wasn't. Of course, if you do better than you expected, a measure also allows you to say, "The program exceeded our expectations."

Examples of Marketing Plans

The marketing plan described in this chapter is a classic textbook example. You don't have to follow this plan exactly, but it's critical that you decide at the beginning what components you will include in the plan and in what order they will appear. Once you have done a few plans and are familiar with the process, you can get them done very quickly, but your first one may take some time. It doesn't have to be overly elaborate; it just needs to include the appropriate information. If you're fortunate enough to be in a library that has its own marketing team, your marketing plan may be more involved. But chances are you're going to be doing marketing in addition to budget, reference, and whatever else you have to do to keep your library running. So it's critical that you become familiar with the format of the plan so that you can create it very quickly.

To get some ideas of great marketing plans, look at the John Cotton Dana awards. Winners are listed in Appendix C. These awards are given by the American Library Association every year and are a competition of librarians and their libraries. They develop marketing projects and plans over the course of a year and then submit them to a committee. This committee selects ten of the best from all different types of libraries. The actual awards are presented at a ceremony during ALA's conference each year. If you would like to see examples of these marketing projects, visit the Web site, at http://www.hwwilson.com/jcdawards/jcdwin2006.htm.

Another example of a marketing plan, from the University of Nevada, Las Vegas, can be seen at http://www.library.unlv.edu/marketing/marketingplan.html. It will give you an idea of the scope and length of a marketing plan. It is two or three years old now, but the library has a marketing goal, to "be recognized by members of the University and the academic community, the citizens of southern Nevada, or anyone here in their classrooms, at home or in their offices . . . ." I'm not saying you want to emulate everything here, but it is an example of a goal, messages to send, responsibilities, key players, procedures and policies, and media contacts. Chapter 3 discusses how to develop media contacts.

Other marketing plans can be found in the resources listed in appendix H, and also look at the examples in Appendix D. Kim Ringler developed one of the plans when she took my marketing course, and she implemented it in the Avon Grove Public Library in West Grove, Pennsylvania. Kim is now the director of that library. The other two plans are from the Abington Library and the Scott Township Public Library. The Scott Township plan includes examples of surveys and flyers.

The next chapter discusses how to use media, newsletters, and annual reports to communicate your library's programs and services to the community.

Chapter 3

Communicate to the Community: Using the Media, Newsletters, and Annual Reports to Market the Library

Libraries should be in the public eye all the time, and it is important to be as visible as possible without spending lots of money on printing and mailing materials. One way for libraries to have access to the community, while spending very little money, is through local media outlets. Most communities have a local newspaper, and many have local radio and television stations, all of which are used by the community to get information. Each of these media outlets is always looking for information that will be of interest to the community. Since the library's resources and programs are offered to community members, the media are usually happy to help get the word out about library activities. Having the media do that for the library is effective in terms of the time, money, and effort saved and in the size of the audience that is reached.

To make the most out of your local media outlets, you need to come up with a *media plan*. The first step in developing the media plan is to determine

- how to get information about your library out to the community (printing, mailing, electronic distribution, or using the media);

- what kind of information should be sent out (programming information, new books and services, bond election information, new personnel, fund-raising information);

- how you are going to distribute the information in advance (instead of just flying around at the last minute trying to figure out who's going to get the information!); and

- when you want to use the media, and how often.

As you think about how to distribute information about your library, you need to decide what kinds of publicity can be handled by the library and what should be handled by local media outlets.

A number of marketing tools are available that you and other librarians may use, including the following:

- Personal contact with users/nonusers (e-mail address, snail-mail address, phone number)

- Internet: Web page, electronic bulletin board, blogs

- Word of mouth

- In-house displays

- Flyers, bookmarks, ads, or coupons that can be placed in

   – books as they circulate,

   – utility bills,

   – local publications,

   – public offices and organizations,

   – school mailings, and

   – organizational publications (school, church, or community newsletters)

The following marketing tools can be used by the media:

- Upcoming programs/calendars of events (summer reading, book discussions, public lectures)

- New materials (weekly book reviews or new acquisitions)

- Feature stories (ways in which the library or librarians have influenced a person or event)

A series of three photographs were turned into posters that were used as in-house displays (see Appendix E). Similar photographs could also be used on flyers, books, or ads.

This chapter covers how your library can develop a plan to work with the media. I show you how to create a media list and how to contact the people who are on your list. Then you'll learn how to create a press release, public service announcement, press kit, and calendar of events. Finally, I give you some useful sources of information that can help your library when working with the media.

Creating a Media List

The first step in creating a media plan is to develop a media list that identifies the newspaper, radio, and television reporters who will publicize information about your library. The list only needs to be created once, but it should be updated by staff members on a regular (at least yearly) basis.

To create your media list, first identify all the local media outlets in your community, such as

> newspapers,
>
> radio stations,
>
> television stations,
>
> school newspapers,
>
> church bulletins, and
>
> community center newsletters.

Next identify the appropriate contact person and contact information for each of these media outlets. Remember to get the following information:

Name

Position

Address

Phone number

Fax number

E-mail address

As you gather this information, it's important to call the organization, rather than rely on information posted on a Web site. Web sites are not always reliable, and this kind of information can change quickly. It is important to identify the person who currently has the responsibilities, rather than the person who was the contact two years ago.

Contacting People on Your Media List

Getting to Know You

Once you have compiled your media list, contact each person on the list. This should be done before you actually need someone to advertise your library's program. Marketing is communication, and you should form a relationship with these media representatives so that they can help you when you need them. After all, wouldn't you much rather talk to somebody you already know?

Here are some things to remember when contacting a media representative:

• Contact the media representative *before* you need him or her.

• Send a letter or e-mail of introduction.

• Follow up with a phone call.

• Do not chat about the weather:

   – have a succinct list of what you want the person to know about your library,

– find out what he or she is interested in covering, and

– determine his or her publishing deadlines.

Getting to Know You Better

Once you have introduced yourself to a media representative, it's time to get to know him or her even better. It's important that you make these representatives feel that you are out for their best interest. If you do this, they will want to cover your library. Following are some things that you need to find out from your media representatives:

- How they prefer to get updates about your library:

  – Press release via e-mail, fax, or mail

  – Phone calls

- How much lead time they need (a month, a week, a day)

Be sure to add all of this information to your media list!

One great way to get to know your media representatives better is to invite them to visit your library. You could invite all of them at one time, but then they wouldn't feel special, so you might want to invite a representative from just one media outlet to come over. Maybe there's something exciting going on in your library that you'd like to invite him or her to see. Or, you could just invite the representative to show up on a regular day so that you can talk to and show him or her the lay of the land.

One thing to remember when you invite media representatives to your library: The photographer won't necessarily come with the interviewer and may not come at all. Have some photos ready to give the interviewer. You may want to find out before the interviewer comes if there are specifications for photos. You may also want to keep a list of photographers in your media list, so that you can call on them if needed.

It also occasionally happens that media representatives say they're coming to cover a special event, and then something happens and they don't show up. They're probably still interested in your event, so your library needs to provide information that the media outlet can use to cover your program. Some of the methods for doing this are press releases, public service announcements, press kits, a calendar of events, and your annual report.

The Press Release

The first media material you'll probably create is a press release. This is a concise document that includes relevant information about your library's new program or service.

You don't want to send a press release about every little thing. You want it to be important so that when media reps see it, you'll have a reputation and they'll know this is something good. If you send press releases for every little thing, they will be ignored. So make sure that when you send a press release, it really is of value.

All the pertinent facts should be included in the first paragraph of the press release, and the entire document should be no longer than one or two pages. A person reading a press release usually reads quickly, looking just for the facts. For this reason, you've got to make it catchy to attract the person's attention, but not so cutesy that you don't include the pertinent information. Here are some things to remember when writing a press release:

- Include only one or two pages that give all the pertinent details.
- Have a title.
- Make the first paragraph catchy and make sure it covers who, what, when, where, and why.
- Stick to the facts.
- Include the library's contact information.
- Include in the last paragraph a boilerplate about the library.

The boilerplate in the very last paragraph should include something interesting about your library that you'd like people to know. It's just a final reminder for people of who you are and where you are coming from.

The press release has to have a standard look to it so that people know it's coming from you. Make sure your library's logo or branding is at the top of the document. Always include the date on the press release, so that media representatives know when the information should be released to the public. Then always provide the contact person, telephone number, and e-mail address, so that if there are any questions, the media representative will be able to go directly to the person in the library who has the information he or she is looking for.

There are other press release standards. At the bottom of the page you should write "for more information" and provide your contact information. At the end of the release put either three pound/number symbols

(# # #) or hyphen-30-hyphen (-30-). If you are going onto two pages, at the end of the first page put the word "more" so that the reader knows there's more on the next page.

The Public Service Announcement

Another kind of media material is the public service announcement, or PSA. It is a short announcement that can be read on radio or television in ten-, thirty-, or sixty-second spots. Often PSAs come on in the early morning on an obscure television station. Nevertheless, you never know who's going to see a PSA, so your library should use PSAs if possible.

To write a PSA, you first need to determine what spots are available. Call people on your media list to see if they have space for PSAs and how long they are. Once you know how much time you have for your public service announcement, you can write it. Make sure you don't include too much information, because you don't want the announcer to speed-read it. You do need to get the pertinent information at the beginning and end of the announcement, because people tend to remember what they hear first and last. Have you ever noticed how in radio announcements they repeat a phone number several times? Various studies indicate that people need to hear something seven to twenty times before they remember it. So make sure the information in your PSA is simple and repeatable. A template for your PSA follows.

Public Service Announcement Template

[Library Logo/Branding: Top of the Page]

[Contact Person Name]

[Contact Person Telephone Number]

[Contact Person Fax Number]

[Contact Person E-mail Address]

[Title of Public Service Announcement]

[Approximate Length of PSA]

[Write the text of your Public Service Announcement here. Remember to keep it simple and repeatable. Don't forget to include the contact information!]

The Press Kit

A press kit is a folder that contains marketing materials about a speaker or event being held in the library. It can be given to media outlets before the event so that they have background information about and photos of the person who will be speaking or the event that will be taking place. For instance, if an author were going to speak at your library, the press kit might include his or her biography, a list of published works, and a photo of that person. You would also include information about your library.

While some press kits can be very involved (especially those from vendors), you don't have to spend a lot of money to create one. The most simple is just a regular folder that you can get for a dollar. Then just print up copies of information that you want the media to know. Put in a brochure for something that's going on or include your annual report or monthly newspaper.

Press kits are a great way to communicate with people on your media list. You may want to have an interview and say that the speaker will be available to the media at a particular time, or you may just want to contact one media representative and say, "I will make this author available to you exclusively." Doing so may sweeten the pot a little bit. You're taking a chance, but if you have established a relationship with your media reps, you'd be surprised at how grateful they may be.

The Calendar of Events

A simple way to advertise programs and events in your library is to post them in a calendar of events. Often local newspapers publish a weekly or monthly calendar. Television and radio stations sometimes have community calendars that they post on their Web sites or announce over the air. Contact the media outlets on your list to see if they have any type of calendar where you can post your library events.

The Annual Report

Annual reports are compilations of circulation statistics, reference statistics, budget allocations, and . . . . Wait a minute! No, they're not!!! Annual reports should be the crown jewel in your marketing array of publications. The annual report should be used to highlight the success experienced at your library during the previous year. The publication can be sent to

>the board of directors,
>
>elected officials in the community,
>
>real estate offices/Welcome Wagon,
>
>library donors,
>
>day care centers,
>
>senior centers,
>
>community centers, and
>
>others.

The report can be made available in print or electronic formats. Print formats can be published in a variety of ways:

>on standard 8½-by-11-inch, 8½-by-14-inch, or 11-by-17-inch paper;
>
>in a tabloid, booklet, trifold, or poster format;
>
>on glossy, colored, or white paper; and
>
>in just black, four-color, or single-color type.

Some libraries have produced coffee-table quality annual reports that have been funded by a donor or institution. Perhaps the local bank or grocery store would underwrite the annual report in exchange for recognition in the publication. The Mt. Lebanon Public Library in Pennsylvania "publishes" its annual report on 5-by-7-inch notepads produced by a local printer. The library's contact information and a different fact about the library are printed on each page.

Examples showing the creative use of text, photographs, and graphics in annual reports are included in Appendix F. Think beyond the stuffy report when you produce the next annual report. Use the report as an opportunity to showcase the library's accomplishments.

Newsletters

Newsletters are an effective way for libraries to communicate with their community of users and nonusers. Newsletters may be produced in-house or with a commercial vendor, or they may be electronic. Newsletter content may focus on upcoming or past events, new acquisitions, a list of donors, and feature stories. A calendar of events is a popular section of most library newsletters.

While it may be costly in terms of staff time and effort and printing and mailing, the benefits of a newsletter are innumerable, including

- distribution and promotion of a calendar of events,

- a focus on new materials or resources,

- features about topics of interest to community members,

- showing support from the community, and

- providing evidence of activities to library funders.

Newsletters can be very effective even if they are not filled with color photos and graphics. Knowing basic design principles can help you produce an in-house publication that is helpful in making your community aware of the library.

As you prepare to create your newsletter, you will have to make some decisions. The steps involved are discussed below.

Step 1: Why Does My Library Need a Newsletter?

The first question you need to answer is why your library needs a newsletter. You must have a compelling reason to publish a newsletter and a list of what you want to include in each issue. If you have decided you definitely wish to publish a newsletter, here are some items you might want to include in it:

a calendar of events,

highlights of new items in the collection,

thanks to donors,

a showcase of past events,

contact information and directions to the library,

materials to reach current library users, and

materials to reach potential library users.

Step 2: Who Will Develop the Newsletter?

The next question concerns the production of the newsletter. Who will be responsible for writing the content and doing the design and layout? Are there staff members or volunteers who have the time and ability to complete it in a timely manner? Once you make the decision to publish a newsletter, you need to ensure that it will be ready on time. What will be included in the newsletter?

- Identify the person(s) responsible for these functions:

  - selecting content,

  - writing and editing, and

  - doing the design and layout.

- Create a library brand and establish a template (see example below) for the newsletter.

Step 3: When and Where Will the Newsletter Be Published?

Decide how often the newsletter should be published and how much it will cost. Do you have the time, money, and material to produce the newsletter on a monthly, quarterly, or semiannual basis?

- Will the newsletter be produced in hard copy?

  - Will it be available in the library?

  - Will it be available in other locations—grocery stores, community centers?

- Will it be mailed?

  - Will it be mailed to library card holders?

  - Will it be mailed to non-library card holders?

- Will it be available electronically on your Web site?

- What will the costs be for

  - producing it,

  - printing it,

  - mailing it, or

  - publishing it electronically?

- Will it be produced

  - monthly,

  - quarterly,

  - semiannually, or

  - at some other frequency?

Step 4: Determining Costs—Printing and Mailing Considerations

Follow the steps indicated for whichever format you choose:

- Printing

  - Decide how many newsletters you will need to have printed.

  - Decide whether the newsletter will be black and white or color. (Many color options are available, so check with your local printer. You may opt to use one color on the front and back pages so that the charge will be less than for using one or more colors on each page.)

  - Will it be printed in-house or commercially?

  - What size will the paper be?

  - What type of paper will be used (glossy, color, newsprint, recycled, etc.)?

  - Decide how many copies will be mailed.

    What are the costs to obtain mailing labels?

    What are the costs for postage?

  - Negotiate with a local printing company for an annual contract.

- Electronic

  - Decide whether the newsletter will be available in print *and* electronic versions *or* electronic only. (What are the advantages and disadvantages of each decision?)

  - How will the newsletter be mounted on the library Web site? Who will prepare the electronic version?

Newsletter Template

- Logo/brand: Determine the "look" that the library wants to project. It can be an established or a new logo. Select the following:

  - Type font that will be used in each newsletter

  - Paper

    White, color, recycled, newsprint

    Size: 8½-by-11, 8½-by-14, 11-by-17, or other

  - Color of ink

- Content:

  - Contact information

  - Calendar of events

  - New acquisitions

  - Photo gallery of events

    speakers

    programs

    National Library Week

    "Teen Tech Week"

    summer reading

    clubs

    Other

  - Special columns

    fun facts

    local history

    technology updates

    other

  - Honor roll of library donors

Many sources are available to help you develop successful newsletters. Sample newsletters can be seen in Appendix G.

Useful Sources

When working with media, you can draw from many useful sources. This section lists some of them to provide an idea of what's out there. The American Library Association, the Association of Research Libraries, and the Medical Library Association all have good, practical, downloadable sites.

American Library Association

Issues and Advocacy, http://www.ala.org/ala/issues/toolsandpub/toolsandpub.htm

Communications Handbook, http://www.ala.org/ala/pio/mediarelationsa/availablepiomat/onlinecommgdAug2006.pdf

Online Media Relations Toolkit, http://www.ala.org/ala/pio/mediarelations/mediarelations.htm

The American Library Association has excellent materials for working with the media. In particular, you should look at their *Communications Handbook for Libraries*. It includes an introductory letter for libraries, which can be customized and sent to your local media outlets. The handbook also gives you information on what media attention can do for the library and tells you how to approach communications so that it doesn't look like you're begging. It gives you hints for how to convince media representatives that you have helpful information that their users, readers, and listeners want.

The ALA also has a section called "Envisioning Your Media Hits." If you have print media, like local magazines and newspapers, you can highlight something as a human interest or feature story, which would be different than just providing information about an event that you are hosting. Sometimes you can write a letter to your editor about something that is happening at your library. Many people read editorials, so this could be another form of publicity for your library. The ALA gives advice on many different types of media hits and helps you think about other ways to advertise your library. Other free items are listed in the subsection "Get Ready, Set, Go! Free Marketing Resources."

Association of Research Libraries

Media Map: Charting A Media Relations Strategy, http://www.arl.org/MediaMap.pdf

The Association of Research Libraries (ARL) has SPEC kits covering best practices for libraries on a variety of topics. They also have professional publications that can be useful when marketing your library. Much of their focus is on management and research libraries, but you may find something helpful. The ARL has produced a smaller publication called a media map. It's only twenty-one pages long, but it's very effective. It talks about building valuable relationships with the media and shows you how to communicate effectively, deliver an effective message, and sell a particular story.

Medical Library Association

Making a Difference: Media Relations, http://www.mlanet.org/publications/tool_kit/media_relate.html

The Medical Library Association, although you may not ordinarily think of it as a resource for public libraries, also has useful media hints. "Making a Difference: Media Relations" is a long toolkit on how to develop fact sheets to work with the media, develop photographs and graphics for the media, and write a photo caption. They also give advice about creating a media list and other media materials. Their suggestions could easily be adapted for your library. If you have little funding, you may be interested in a list of free items.

Ready, Set, Go! Free Marketing Resources

ALA: @ Your Library, http://www.ala.org/@yourlibrary

Users can access information about the @ Your Library Campaign, including recent news and participating libraries as well as detailed information about related campaigns (including the ACRL Academic & Research Library Campaign, the PLA Smartest Card Campaign, the ALSC Kids! Campaign, the AASL School Library Campaign, and the Campaign for World's Libraries). Logos in multiple languages can be downloaded, and a "PR Tools and Resources" section provides users with access to free PSAs (in both print and video formats), slogans, bookmarks, artwork andphotography, and communications tools, including sample press materials and "Facts & Figures" handouts.

ALA Public Programs Office (PPO), http://www.ala.org/ala/ppo/ publicprograms.htm

The ALA PPO provides leadership, training, resources, and networking opportunities that can help librarians host cultural experiences for patrons. This Web site provides news and information about available grants, awards, traveling exhibitions, current PPO programs, and programs of interest from PPO partners. Information on grant writing is provided in detail, and the Web site also hosts an "Online Resource Center," which provides resources, guides, and models free of charge.

ALA Resources, http://www.ala.org/ala/ourassociation/offices/ offices.htm

"Offices" are units of the ALA that address broad interests and issues of concern to ALA members and the general public. Examples are the Office of Diversity, the Office of Intellectual Freedom, and the Office for Literacy and Outreach Services.

Cognotes, http://www.ala.org/ala/eventsandconferences/midwinter/2007/cognotes. htm

This daily newsletter from the ALA's 2007 Midwinter Conference highlights each day's events, sessions, opportunities, ideas, and relevant news.

Library Media & PR, http://www.ssdesign.com/librarypr/

This Web site contains a "Little Black Book" of useful marketing contacts, an annotated list of PR or marketing competitions that librarians can enter, and a searchable collection of library media and PR-specific articles. A "Toolbox" feature contains free clip art, symbols, Web site banners, bookmarks, and links to other resources, including tips for public librarians who are designing Web sites. Current visitors to the Web site can view a podcast on publicity and PR for promoting a summer reading program at a library.

Market the Future, http://www.fearless-future.com/wordpress/

This trendy blog highlights hip visual marketing ideas for libraries from a more commercial sphere.

Market Your Library from Gale, http://www.galegroup.com/freestuff/
index.htm

This Web site provides downloadable marketing materials (in PDF
format) for individuals who work at academic, military, hospital,
school, public, and law libraries. Available resources include templates,
bookmarks, postcards, fliers, print ads, radio scripts, multilingual school
resources, and thank-you cards. Users can also access mailing list resources and U.S. Postal Service guidelines.

Marketing Best Practices Wiki, http://www.libsuccess.org/index.php?title=
Marketing

This wiki takes the very best library marketing resources and ideas
available on the Web and makes them available at one convenient site.
Links and ideas are available on almost every conceivable aspect of li-
brarianship.

Marketing Treasures, http://www.chrisolson.com/marketingtreasures/

This free monthly electronic newsletter is written for market-
ing-oriented information professionals, and its current and past issues
can be accessed via e-mail (in plain text or HTML) or at the Web site (in
PDF). A special "Resources" section of the Web site features annotated
lists of additional Web sites on topics such as marketing, vendor relations, library advocacy, and e-catalogs.

MLANet Media Relations—Helpful for Medical Libraries, http://www.
mlanet.org/publications/tool_kit/media_relate.html

This media relations Web site provides valuable information about
putting together a media list, providing background, and compiling and
using a press kit. Samples of queries, news releases, photo alerts, fact
sheets, photo captions, and information Rx are provided, as well as a
media contact form.

Handling Bad Press

Before ending this chapter, I'd like to address how you handle bad
press. In the event of bad press, you should have a person in the library
who is designated as the contact for the media. This person should be in

direct contact with the director or the library board so that the right messages—and not conflicting messages—are getting out. You should instruct all other staff members to direct media representatives to that person, if their questions are about something that's affecting the library. A response to bad press doesn't always have to be immediate; you can simply say that a statement will be released or you will talk to the media at a specific time. That way, the library has a chance to prepare what it would like to convey to the media. Remember that bad press isn't always such an awful thing, because sometimes you can make it into lemonade and turn the situation around.

The next chapter discusses fund-raising.

Chapter 4

Fund-Raising

An effective marketing plan includes information about how you will fund your program or service. To successfully fund your library marketing projects, you'll have to be able to effectively develop relationships with potential donors. This chapter focuses on some ways you can raise support for and promote the library in your community through the networking that is done by library staff and Friends groups. You can also raise funds for the library by developing grant proposals to state and federal agencies, foundations, and private donors.

Developing Relationships

People in your community should be reminded (or told) about the services and resources that are offered by the library. Librarians need to make the library and themselves known to the public, rather than waiting for people to come into the library. People are willing to contribute to causes that are important to them, and librarians must find ways to let people know what is happening in the library. You may not realize it, but you can develop many relationships when working in a library. Every contact has the potential to place the library in the public view and to increase support. Think of ways that the people you deal with on a daily basis could have an impact on the library.

The following relationships can provide opportunities for librarians to reach out beyond the library doors. Take some time to think of how these could benefit the library.

> Librarians and patrons
>
> Librarians and staff
>
> Librarians and the board of trustees
>
> Librarians and the media
>
> Librarians and funders
>
> Librarians and nonusers
>
> Librarians and volunteers
>
> Librarians and Friends groups

All of these relationships can be used, in different ways, to raise funds for your library. As you develop your marketing plan, keep these relationships in mind. The relationships that you have developed can be called upon to help fund your program when the need arises.

Local Funding

The potential to find funding for your project can be within the local community, and you should be prepared to make contacts with each encounter. Your library staff should be ready to give an "elevator speech" whenever the opportunity arises. As mentioned previously, an "elevator speech" is used when you have a brief opportunity to tell someone about the highlights of your project or organization—in the time it would take to reach your destination in an elevator. Many librarians are prepared with interesting facts about library programs or services that can be told quickly to someone while they are riding in an elevator, standing in line at the grocery store, or attending a social gathering. Having short "stories" ready to share with anyone you meet is a great way to spread the news about what the library is doing. You may miss great fund-raising opportunities if you stand silently during an elevator ride!

Take some time to select key points about your library and to ask your staff for ideas that you could share with others. Following are examples of talking points for elevator speeches:

- Last summer _____ children participated in the summer reading program and they read ___ books.

- We deliver ___ books to seniors in the nursing facility each week.

- The library is working with the hospital to give books to the families of each newborn, and we invite them to the baby lapsit program in the library. Did you know that reading to babies increases the literacy rate of children?

- _____ cans of food were collected for the food bank during our campaign to return overdue books. Fines were cancelled when the books were returned with a contribution of food.

In each of these exchanges the librarian should be ready to give out a business card with the name, address, phone number, and Web site of the library so the person can contact the library for more information. Also, be ready to tell about the exciting plans the library has for future projects. Get your new contacts interested in the library, and have specific projects ready for them to provide assistance.

Friends of the Library

Friends of the Library groups are volunteers who can play major roles in marketing libraries to their communities and helping a library to achieve its strategic goals. These groups are vital to public, school, and academic libraries in their efforts to increase visibility and assist in fund-raising. Fund-raising efforts sponsored by Friends groups include a wide variety of events:

> book sales,
>
> art auctions,
>
> photo contests (with winning photos depicted on library calendars that are sold to the public),
>
> high teas,
>
> galas,
>
> book signings,

theatrical productions,

Chinese/silent auctions,

prepackaged food sales,

restaurant "library nights" (10 percent of sales goes to the library),

selling bricks,

kiddie carnivals,

cookbook sales,

booths or raffles at a larger event,

bell ringers on street corners,

a "Poor Man's Dinner,"

wine and cheese events,

dessert parties,

selling gear with the library logo,

paid services or events,

flea market booths,

bingo/poker nights with buy-in, and

"Read-a-Thons."

FOLUSA (Friends of the Library USA) provides a comprehensive resource for Friends' groups, including valuable materials on how to engage in effective fund-raising efforts. Examples of the fund-raising efforts of Friends of the Library groups are available at their Web site (http://folusa.org).

Grants

Librarians have a solid record of writing successful grant proposals to obtain funding for projects. The ability to locate appropriate funding sources and the skills needed to develop grant proposals are easy to learn, and funds are available from private donors, foundations, and the government.

State and Federal Funding

Public librarians should be aware of federal funds that are available through the Grants to States program using a population-based formula. Funding from the Library Services and Technology Act (LSTA) is provided to the state library administrative agencies to support library efforts to

- expand services for learning and access to information and educational resources in a variety of formats, in all types of libraries, for individuals of all ages;

- develop library services that provide all users access to information through local, state, regional, national, and international electronic networks;

- provide electronic and other linkages between and among all types of libraries;

- develop public and private partnerships with other agencies and community-based organizations;

- target library services to individuals of diverse geographic, cultural, and socioeconomic backgrounds, to individuals with disabilities, and to individuals with limited functional literacy or information skills; and

- target library and information services to persons having difficulty using a library and to underserved urban and rural communities, including children from families with incomes below the poverty line.

Information about LSTA grants and other federal and state awards is available on the Web site of each state library. You should develop a relationship with the appropriate representative from your state library to learn about the funding that is available to support projects for your library. Following is a list of Web sites for each state:

Alabama: http://www.apls.state.al.us

Alaska: http://library.state.ak.us

Arizona: http://www.lib.az.us

Arkansas: http://www.asl.lib.ar.us

California: http://www.library.ca.gov

Colorado: http://www.cde.state.co.us/index_library.htm

Connecticut: http://www.cslib.org

Delaware: http://www.state.lib.de.us

Florida: http://dlis.dos.state.fl.us/index.cfm

Georgia: http://www.georgialibraries.org

Hawaii: http://www.librarieshawaii.org/

Idaho: http://libraries.idaho.gov/

Illinois: http://www.cyberdriveillinois.com/departments/library/
home.html

Indiana: http://www.statelib.lib.in.us

Iowa: http://www.silo.lib.ia.us

Kansas: http://www.skyways.org/KSL/

Kentucky: http://www.kdla.ky.gov

Louisiana: http://www.state.lib.la.us

Maine: http://www.maine.gov/msl/

Maryland: http://www.marylandpublicschools.org/MSDE/
divisions/library/

Massachusetts: http://mblc.state.ma.us/

Michigan: http://www.michigan.gov/hal

Minnesota: http://education.state.mn.us/mde/Learning_
Support/Library_Services_and_School_Technology/
index.html

Mississippi: http://www.mlc.lib.ms.us

Missouri: http://www.sos.mo.gov/library

Montana: http://msl.mt.gov/

Nebraska: http://www.nlc.state.ne.us/

Nevada: http://www.nevadaculture.org

New Hampshire: http://www.nh.gov/nhsl

New Jersey: http://www.njstatelib.org

New Mexico: http://www.stlib.state.nm.us

New York: http://www.nysl.nysed.gov

North Carolina: http://statelibrary.dcr.state.nc.us

North Dakota: http://ndsl.lib.state.nd.us

Ohio: http://winslo.state.oh.us

Oklahoma: http://www.odl.state.ok.us

Oregon: http://oregon.gov/OSL

Pennsylvania: http://www.statelibrary.state.pa.us

Rhode Island: http://www.olis.ri.gov/

South Carolina: http://www.statelibrary.sc.gov/

South Dakota: http://www.sdstatelibrary.com

Tennessee: http://www.tennessee.gov/tsla/

Texas: http://www.tsl.state.tx.us

Utah: http://library.utah.gov/

Vermont: http://dol.state.vt.us

Virginia: http://www.lva.lib.va.us

Washington: http://www.secstate.wa.gov/library/

West Virginia: http://www.librarycommission.lib.wv.us

Wisconsin: http://dpi.wi.gov/dltcl/index.html

Wyoming: http://www-wsl.state.wy.us

Foundations

A foundation is a charitable organization created by individuals or institutions for the purpose of distributing funds to support specific areas of interest. The best source for libraries to identify charitable institutions is the publications of the Foundation Center (http://www.foundationcenter.org).

The national Foundation Center is located in New York City, with branches located in several libraries in larger cities across the country. In addition, the Foundation Center supports "Cooperating Collections," which are housed in libraries, community foundations, and other non-profit resource centers throughout the United States. These resource centers provide a core of Foundation Center publications and supplementary materials useful in the grant-seeking process. Each Foundation Center has access to all the resources of the main center in New York, so check to find the one that is closest to you. The Foundation Center has a subscription database, *The Foundation Directory Online*, that includes 80,000 grantmakers and 500,000 different grants. Accessing this database will allow you to identify potential foundations whose funding interests match those of your library project.

Corporate Funding, Corporate Foundations, and Local Businesses

Corporations often have a related foundation that is designed for philanthropic or charitable giving. It is important to identify corporations that have philanthropic interests that match the needs of your library. Again, you can identify corporations that have giving interests similar to those of your library project by consulting the Foundation Center (http://www.foundationcenter.org).

Example: A library in an ethnically diverse community developed a marketing plan that celebrates the cultures of the various groups. The activities included an artist series that features lectures, an art show, and artists-in-residence. Through the Foundation Center the library identified Wachovia as a likely corporate sponsor. Wachovia's funding priorities (as identified on their Web site, located through the Foundation Center) focus on arts and culture, with primary goals to

- facilitate access to and participation in cultural experiences for persons with low to moderate income and

- ensure the availability of a broad array of artistic opportunities or venues that reflect the diversity of the community.

The library could develop a proposal to Wachovia that reflects the goals of the corporation and the needs of the library. The possibilities are limitless—all librarians need is the knowledge of where to search for potential funding!

A formal grant proposal is not always needed to obtain corporate funding. Often you may contact the organization by phone or e-mail to ask about corporate sponsorship for a library project or activity. Corporations and local businesses may partner with a library in several ways:

- through capital support:

    - funding to support the project;

- through in-kind contributions of

    - equipment or

    - supplies;

- through marketing and advertising support:

    – providing advertisements in return for placement of the corporate logo on materials;

- through employee involvement:

    – employee volunteers for projects; and

- through networking opportunities with business associates:

    – referrals to other organizations that can provide support.

Following are some examples:

- A local grocer might provide snacks for an after-school homework program in return for

    – acknowledgment in the library or library publications or

    – a sign in the store advertising: Proud Sponsor of Library After-School Program.

- A business will provide money or in-kind contributions for a program in return for

    – acknowledgment in the library or library publications or

    – a sign in the business establishment advertising: Proud Sponsor of Library Program.

- A library develops a Sponsor Hall of Fame that is displayed in the library, in library publications, and on posters.

Private Donors and Benefactors

Contributions from individuals are common to libraries. Many public libraries were made possible through individual contributions of property and collections, and many are located in houses donated by citizens of the community. There are many examples of the ways in which private donors contribute to the growth of libraries.

Libraries can set up formal giving programs for the general public, and they may also establish relationships with individuals who have special collections or interests in supporting the library. Consider

a benefactor program with established levels of giving;

contributions to commemorate birthdays, special events, and memorials;

bequests or planned giving; and

a capital campaign for a specified project (furniture, technology, building, etc.).

Electronic Fund-Raising Resources

The following resources provide basic information about fund-raising for libraries:

Funding and Grant Sources, http://www.libraryhq.com/funding.html

Fund-raising for Libraries, http://www.librarysupportstaff.com/find$.html

Webjunction: An online community for library staff—Web page on fund-raising, http://www.webjunction.org/do/Navigation?category=328

ALA Library Fund-raising: Selected Annotated Bibliography, http://www.ala.org/library/fact24.html

Library Fund-raising on the Web: A Practical Guide for Libraries, http://www.lights.com/how-to/libraries.html

Association of Fund-raising Professionals, http://www.nsfre.org/

Foundation in a Box, http://foundationinabox.org/guide

There are many more ways in which your library could participate in fund-raising activities than you might think. Your creativity will help you expand your original list.

Putting It All Together

The material and examples provided here are intended to get you started increasing the visibility of your library. Remember that communication is the key to effective marketing. Make the most of each opportunity presented to you.

Appendix A

Nominal Group Technique

The Friends of the Library decided to participate in a nominal group technique (NGT) exercise in preparation for determining the type of fund-raising project that would appeal to a broad audience. The director sent this notice to each of the ten members of the Friends of the Library:

> On Friday morning we will meet together from 9 to 11 a.m. in the conference room to identify potential fund-raising options. Please bring a list of all the fund-raising ideas that you have received from library patrons or that you think would be interesting to people in our community who are loyal patrons and to those who have not used the library.
>
> Coffee and bagels will be available beginning at 8:45 a.m.

Step 1: Identify the facilitator prior to the announcement of the date. This can be anyone who knows the NGT process and can keep the group on target. Gather materials the day before the NGT session: flipcharts, Post-it™ notes or index cards and tape.

Step 2: By 8:30 a.m. have room set up with coffee and bagels, materials, and seating for everyone

Step 3: At 9:00 a.m., the facilitator should ask the participants to take their seats and explain that they are going to take part in a process to determine the best fund-raising projects for the library.

Step 4: The facilitator gives everyone a paper that repeats the purpose of the process—to identify potential fund-raising options—and asks the participants to write their ideas on the paper:

- **Round 1:** The facilitator asks each person to share one idea that will be written on the flipchart so that everyone can see it. There will be NO discussion allowed—only the generation of ideas.

- **Round 2:** Same as round 1. A person may "pass" if he or she does not have an idea, and the facilitator will move on to the next person.

- **Round 3:** Same as round 1; however, each person is asked even if he or she "passed" in the previous round because he or she may have thought of an idea.

Each person shares one idea per round. The facilitator writes each idea on the flipchart and numbers it in consecutive order. The rounds are continued until all of the ideas have been generated.

Example:

The Friends of the Library who are participating in the nominal group technique are:

Bud	Sarah	Doris
John	Tom	Carolyn
Theresa	Ron	Marcy
Chris		

In **round 1** the following suggestions are made:

Bud: book sale

John: art auction

Theresa: photo contest (with winning photos depicted on library calendars to be sold to the public)

Chris: high tea

Sarah: gala

Tom: banquet

Ron: book signing

Doris: theatrical production

Carolyn: Chinese/silent auction

Marcy: Prepackaged food sales

In **round 2** the following suggestions are made:

Bud: restaurant "library night" (10 percent of sales goes to the library)

John: "pass"

Theresa: selling bricks

Chris: kiddie carnival

Sarah: cookbook sales

Tom: "pass"

Ron: booth or raffle at a larger event

Doris: bell ringers on street corners

Carolyn: gala

Marcy: "Poor Man's Dinner"

In **round 3** the following suggestions are made:

Bud: "pass"

John: wine and cheese event

Theresa: dessert party

Chris: selling gear with library logo

Sarah: "pass"

Tom: "pass"

Ron: paid services or events

Doris: flea market booth

Carolyn: "pass"

Marcy: "pass"

In **round 4** the following suggestions are made:

Bud: bingo/poker night with buy-in

John: "pass"

Theresa: "Read-a-Thons"

Chris: "pass"

Sarah: "pass"

Tom: "pass"

Ron: "pass"

Doris: "pass"

Carolyn: "Pass"

Marcy: "pass"

In **round 5** no one has any suggestions.

The facilitator writes each idea on the flipchart, which looks like this:

1. book sale

2. art auction

3. photo contest (with winning photos depicted on library calendars that are sold to the public)

4. high tea

5. gala

6. book signing

7. theatrical production

8. Chinese/silent auction

9. prepackaged food sales

10. restaurant "library night" (10 percent of sales goes to the library)

11. selling bricks

12. kiddie carnival

13. cookbook sales

14. booth or raffle at a larger event

15. bell ringers on street corners

16. gala

17. "Poor Man's Dinner"

18. wine and cheese event

19. dessert party

20. selling gear w/library logo

21. paid services or events

22. flea market booth

23. bingo/poker night with buy-in

24. "Read-a-Thons"

Step 5: Each idea is reviewed and explained by someone who did *not* make the original suggestion. The idea may be discussed openly after it has been explained to the satisfaction of the person who suggested it.

Example:

- It is pointed out that the suggestion to have a "gala" (numbers 5 and 16) was listed two times, so number 16 is removed from the list.

- The group discusses the similarity between number 14 (booth or raffle) and number 22 (flea market booth) but decides to keep the ideas separate rather than combining them.

- The group decides that the silent auction could be held at any event, but they would vote separately for it.

Step 6:

- Each individual selects the five suggestions that he or she likes best and writes the suggestion on either an index card or a Post-it ™ note.

- The individual ranks the five suggestions and places the ranked order on the card, 5 being the highest number of "points" and 1 being the lowest number of "points."

- The anonymous ballots are either "stuck" beside the corresponding idea on the flipchart or board or the index cards are collected and tallied.

- Those suggestions with the highest scores are then acted upon by the group or submitted to another group for further action.

Example:

Each person "sticks" his or her five ballots beside the corresponding idea on the flipchart. This provides a visual representation of the anonymous voting so that no one can say justifiably that his or her suggestion wasn't selected even though "everyone was in favor of it!" The results listed below indicate the number of people (votes) who select each of the suggestions and the sum of the points that they awarded. The suggestions that receive the largest number of votes and the highest number of points narrow the original list from twenty-four to eight. The group can then focus on how to plan for these events. Their decision could result in another NGT or general discussion, or these results could be submitted to another planning group. (Top votes are in boldface type.)

1. **book sale (5 votes/20 points)**

2. art auction (2 votes/6 points)

3. photo contest (with winning photos depicted on library calendars that are sold to the public)

4. high tea (1 vote/1 point)

5. **gala (9 votes/40 points)**

6. **book signing (8 votes/38 points)**

7. theatrical production (0 votes/0 points)

8. **Chinese/silent auction (10 votes/43 points)**

9. prepackaged food sales (1 vote/2 points)

10. **restaurant "library night" (10 percent of sales goes to the library) (8 votes/25 points)**

11. selling bricks (1 vote/2 points)

12. kiddie carnival (2 votes/6 points)

13. cookbook sales (2 votes/8 points)

14. **booth or raffle at a larger event (9 votes/17 points)**

15. bell ringers on street corners

16. ~~Gala~~

17. "Poor Man's Dinner" (1 vote/3 points)

18. **wine and cheese event (6 votes/21 points)**

19. dessert party (2 votes/5 points)

20. selling gear w/library logo (3 votes/3 points)

21. paid services or events (2 votes/7 points)

22. flea market booth (4 votes/8 points)

23. bingo/poker night with buy-in (1 vote/5 points)

24. **"Read-a-Thons" (8 votes/25 points)**

Appendix B

Boilerplate Example

Prepared by Sara Gillespie

Located in Anytown, Anystate, the Anytown Public Library serves a population of 20,000 with a collection of 200,000 items including books, magazines and media. Our staff serves our citizens from 12:00 p.m. to 8:00 p.m. weekdays and from 12:00 to 6:00 on Saturday and Sunday. With an annual circulation of 200,000, representing 100 items per capita, our specialized collections serve approximately 1,000 non-English speakers with four language materials, Chinese, Japanese, Spanish, and Vietnamese. We offer access to ten major databases and access to 24/7 reference service.

Storytimes are offered for lapsits and preschoolers, and our children's department provides an exciting summer reading program for 1,000 children each summer. Our after-school programs serve 8,000 students in grades 4 to 12. Contact Mary Jones at 111-222-3333 or mjones@anytown.org.

Appendix C

John Cotton Dana Library Public Relations Award Winners, 2007–2002

Prepared by Elisa McClain

All URLS were accessed June 7, 2007.

2007 Winners

Brooklyn Public Library (Brooklyn, NY), http://www.brooklynpubliclibrary.org/
Annotation from LAMA: Brooklyn Public Library in Brooklyn, N.Y., for "Brooklyn Reads to Babies." This model early literacy program, with appealing multilingual materials, had the ambitious goal of reaching every family in Brooklyn. Combining research, outreach through more than 30 strategic partners, and creative use of appropriate communication tools led to a tremendously successful PR campaign with measurable results.

Douglas County Libraries (Castle Rock, CO), http://www.douglascountylibraries.org/
Annotation from LAMA: Douglas County Libraries in Castle Rock, Colo., for "Page to Stage Productions." The library used the unique power of live theater connected with children's literature as an outreach tool. A professional production based on James Marshall's popular book *Miss Nelson Is Missing* reached over 10,000 children in schools and libraries throughout the county, driving up summer reading participation by 10 percent and doing it all for a cost of less than $1 per audience member.

Huntsville-Madison County Public Library (Huntsville, AL), http://hpl.lib.al.us/

Annotation from LAMA: Huntsville-Madison County Public Library, Huntsville, Ala., for their public relations campaign promoting The Big Read: Huntsville Reads "The Great Gatsby." The library's thoughtful, comprehensive, and well-executed campaign used multiple public relations strategies, including community partnerships, to target diverse audiences. Their efforts resulted in renewed interest and enthusiasm for their "one book" program by the community and the media, and achieved a dramatic increase in participation over the previous year's project.

Milner Library at Illinois State University (Normal, IL), http://www.library.ilstu.edu/

Annotation from LAMA: Milner Library at Illinois State University in Normal, Ill., for "Honoring Illinois State University's First Librarian Angeline 'Ange' Vernon Milner." This extensive public awareness campaign brought new life to a legendary library ghost on the 150th anniversary of her birth. A public relations effort refocused local perception, transforming the legend of a very real leader in the library profession from a campus ghost haunting the collections to the groundbreaking professional and scholar she was.

Ocean County Library (Toms River, NJ), http://www.oceancountylibrary.org/

Annotation from LAMA: Ocean County Library, Toms River, N.J., for "Hurricane Katrina—Partners in Caring." In immediate response to the devastation, Ocean County Library raised more than $120,000 in cash to help restore services and established a lifelong bond with the Hancock County Library in Mississippi. Using a variety of creative methods and an aggressive public relations campaign, Ocean County's initiative and outreach brought staff of both libraries and the two shore communities together to make a difference.

The Office of Commonwealth Libraries (Harrisburg, PA), http://www.statelibrary.state.pa.us/libraries/site/default.asp

Annotation from LAMA: The Office of Commonwealth Libraries in Harrisburg, Pa., for "Pennsylvania: One Book, Every One Child," a comprehensive statewide campaign to reach 560,000 preschool children, [which] provided stimulating literacy experiences and encouraged lifelong learning. The program donated the charming book *Inside Mouse, Outside Mouse* to 641 public libraries and 15,000 early care and education programs. Additional supporting resources included author visits, a museum trunk, print materials, and a resource Web site.

The Wyoming State Library (Cheyenne, WY), http://www-wsl.state.wy.us/

Annotation from LAMA: The Wyoming State Library in Cheyenne, Wyo., for their statewide campaign, "Wyoming Libraries: Bringing the World to Wyoming," involving every library in the state. This highly creative and visually expressive public awareness campaign combines Wyoming lore and cowboy culture with global literary and travel icons—a windmill atop the Eiffel Tower fills a watering trough for grazing cattle—raising the profile of the library to statewide administrators and lonesome cowboys, as well.

2006 Winners

Calgary Public Library (Calgary, Alberta, Canada), http://calgarypubliclibrary.com/

Annotation from LAMA: Calgary Public Library (Calgary, Alberta, Canada), for their innovative and unique program "The Great Alberta Reading Challenge." Calgary Public Library invited all libraries across the province to join in a friendly competition with prizes for the highest participation.

Charleston County Public Library (Charleston, SC), http://www.ccpl.org/

Annotation from LAMA: Charleston County Public Library (Charleston, SC), for its innovative project, "Remembering the Cooper River Bridges," an aggressive public relations effort with local media partnerships, which dramatically increased the public's awareness of the significance of Charleston's bridges, and raised the library's public profile with nearly $800,000 in free news coverage.

The James B. Duke Library-Furman University (Greenville, SC), http://library.furman.edu/about/jbduke.htm

Annotation from LAMA: The James B. Duke Library— Furman University (Greenville, SC), for "ICU: Life in the Library" and "Year of the Library," a two-phase building renovation and expansion campaign. Staff members injected a humorous medical theme to ease stress during the construction phase, which was followed by a yearlong celebration of the library, its new building, and [its] capabilities.

Loudoun County Public Library (Leesburg, VA), http://www.lcpl.lib.va.us/branches.htm

Examples of programming (from CD and handout):

    1.   More than 1,500 T-shirts were distributed to students who attended the National Library Week Program featuring Chris

Crutcher, presented by the Loudoun County (VA) Public Library.

2. Loudoun County (VA) Public Library 2005 One Book-One Community author Karen Hesse met and spoke with students, teachers, and fans. More than 12,000 copies of her One Book-One Community book *Witness* were given away to the community during September and October.

3. Through a MetLife Foundation/Libraries for the Future Grant (*Literacy Through Photography*), students in Loudoun County (VA) Mental Health, Mental Retardation's Homework Club worked with the library on the project.

4. Through a grant awarded to the Loudoun County (VA) Public Library, writer Luis J. Rodriguez (author of *Always Running La Vida Loca: Gang Days in L.A.*) presented programs at the Loudoun County (VA) Public Library, Juvenile Detention Center, and in the community.

5. Morris Dees, Cofounder of the Southern Poverty Law Center, spoke to 900 community members as part of the Loudoun County (VA) Public Library 2005 One Book-One Community.

6. Summer reading volunteers assisted the Loudoun County (VA) Public Library Outreach Services delivery to Senior Residential Centers in the area.

7. Teen READ Week was held.

8. Teens helped design the 4,000-square-foot Teen Center that will be added to the Rust (Leesburg) Library, a branch of the Loudoun County (VA) Public Library.

9. "After Hours Teen Center" was held. Teens participated in programs, activities, or just "hanging out" in a safe, enriching environment. Attendance was 100+ each Friday evening.

10. Teens at the "After Hours Teen Center" gave their ideas on what they would like to do at the library

Annotation from LAMA: Loudoun County Public Library (Leesburg, VA), for their program "Hanging Out Rocks!", a campaign that responded to the needs of teens in their growing county by giving them a place that they could call their own. Teen participation, and the many strategies utilized in this thoroughly analyzed and detailed public relations plan, [were] key to moving the campaign forward and led to additional resources granted for a popular after-hours teen center at the library where "Hanging Out Rocks!"

Public Library of Charlotte and Mecklenburg County (Charlotte, NC), http://plcmc.org/

Annotation from LAMA: Public Library of Charlotte and Mecklenburg County (Charlotte, NC), for "Bringing the Story to Life," a campaign to celebrate the opening of ImaginOn, an innovative new space that combines a library and children's theater. Staff overcame a number of hurdles, including some last-minute negative publicity, and responded with a magnificent public relations effort that resulted in attendance and media coverage at their grand opening events exceeding all expectations.

The Public Library of Cincinnati and Hamilton County (Cincinnati, OH), http://www.cincinnatilibrary.org/

Annotation from LAMA: The Public Library of Cincinnati and Hamilton County (Cincinnati, OH), for a dynamic and comprehensive library card sign-up campaign. In partnership with the Cincinnati Zoo and Botanical Garden, the campaign used a fun and appealing wildlife theme with multilayered marketing strategies to reach and motivate students county-wide to sign up for library cards. The campaign resulted in record sign-ups, increased awareness of library services, and [created] invaluable community and media relationships.

2005 Winners

Calgary Public Library (Calgary, Alberta, Canada), http://calgarypubliclibrary.com/

Annotation from LAMA: Calgary Public Library (Calgary, Alberta, Canada), for "Rediscover Your Public Library." This highly researched and well-planned campaign used imagination and humor to target specific audiences and convert library awareness to increased library use.

The Louisiana Center for the Book in the State Library of Louisiana (Baton Rouge, LA), http://www.state.lib.la.us/la_dyn_templ.cfm?doc_id=113

Annotation from LAMA: The Louisiana Center for the Book in the State Library of Louisiana (Baton Rouge, LA), for its comprehensive campaign, "Louisiana Book Festival," a free, family- oriented celebration of writers, reading, and books. Community partnerships, activities galore, and extensive media coverage contributed to increased awareness of Louisiana's rich literary heritage.

Maricopa County Library District (Phoenix, AZ), http://www.mcldaz.org
Annotation from LAMA: Maricopa County Library District (Phoenix, AZ), for "The Mystery Club of Luna Drive," an online young adult novel that gives teens an opportunity to solve a mystery using puzzles, ciphers, and critical thinking.

North Suburban Library System (Wheeling, IL), http://www.nsls.info/
Annotation from LAMA: North Suburban Library System (Wheeling, IL), for outstanding positioning of libraries as centers of critical community services. Their innovative partnership with the League of Women Voters inspired more than 80 participating libraries to provide voter registration service through their program "Honor September 11: Register to Vote @ Your Library."

The Riverside County Library System (Riverside, CA), http://www.riverside.lib.ca.us/riverside/
Annotation from LAMA: The Riverside County Library System (Riverside, CA), for its innovative project, "Leer Es Triunfar—Reading Is Succeeding," designed to increase the awareness and use of library services among Latino residents in Riverside County through a series of public programs, community events, celebrity television spots, and targeted Spanish-language publications.

San Diego State University Library & Information Access (San Diego, CA), http://infodome.sdsu.edu/
Annotation from LAMA: San Diego State University Library & Information Access (San Diego, CA), for "Spirit of the Land Environmental Symposium and Gala Dinner." This collaboration with the Viejas Band of Kumeyaay Indians assembled nationally known authors, scientists, and environmentalists to engage in two days of discussion open to the public and garnered support for the library's environmental collections.

The Seattle Public Library (Seattle, WA), http://www.spl.org/
Annotation from LAMA: The Seattle Public Library (Seattle, WA), for the grand-opening celebration of its internationally acclaimed central library. Part of a multi-year program to improve the Seattle Public Library system, the "Libraries for All" program brought public library awareness to an unprecedented level.

2004 Winners

Barrington Area Library (Barrington, IL), http://www. barringtonarealibrary.org/

Annotation from LAMA: Barrington Area Library, Barrington, Illinois, for "Simple Living," a series of lifestyle programs featuring the concept of paring down, making choices, and staying focused, designed in response to the changing economic climate.

Dr. Martin Luther King, Jr. Library (San Jose, CA), http://www. sjlibrary.org/about/locations/king/index.htm

Annotation from LAMA: Dr. Martin Luther King, Jr. Library, San Jose, California, for a building dedication campaign, highlighting a groundbreaking partnership between the San Jose State University and the city's public library.

Edmon Low Library, Oklahoma State University (Stillwater, OK), http://www.library.okstate.edu/

Annotation from LAMA: Edmon Low Library, Oklahoma State University, Stillwater, Oklahoma, for a stellar commemorative celebration entitled "That Was Then . . . This Is Now," focusing on the successes and challenges marking 50 years of building pride.

Halifax Public Libraries (Dartmouth, Nova Scotia, Canada), http://www.halifaxpubliclibraries.ca/

Annotation from LAMA: Halifax Public Libraries, Dartmouth, Nova Scotia, for its complex and layered "Summer Reading Quest," featuring seven fantasy characters in an original, interactive adventure, and a dynamic Web site designed to attract the reluctant reader.

Las Vegas-Clark County Library District (Las Vegas, NV), http://www.lvccld.org/index.cfm

Annotation from LAMA: Las Vegas-Clark County Library District, Las Vegas, Nevada, for "Reading Las Vegas, Books: A Sure Bet!"—a catchy public relations and branding campaign using casino imagery to promote the library's second annual adult reading program.

Orange County Public Library (Santa Ana, CA), http://www.ocpl.org/

Annotation from LAMA: Orange County Public Library, Santa Ana, California, for the imaginative Egyptology Lecture Series—a program of scholars and other luminaries that was developed from a unique partnership with the American Research Center in Egypt.

The Pioneer Library System (Norman, OK), http://www.pioneer.lib. ok.us/

Annotation from LAMA: The Pioneer Library System, Norman, Oklahoma, for an intriguing and visually appealing campaign that promoted libraries as prominent cultural agents. The Red Dirt Book Festival celebrated the Oklahoma literary experience.

2003 Winners

The Genesee District Library (Flint, MI), http://www.thegdl.org/
Annotation from LAMA: The Genesee District Library, Flint, Mich., for opening a 3,800-square-foot demonstration location inside a busy shopping center to take their services to the people. Since their initial opening, this new location has averaged over 7,000 visitors per month and registered over 2,000 new cardholders.

Guernsey Memorial Library (Norwich, NY), http://www.4cls.org/ webpages/members/norwich/NORWICH.html
Annotation from LAMA: Guernsey Memorial Library, Norwich, N.Y., for a delightful celebration of the library's Centennial anniversary. The celebration focused on genealogy, local architecture, and history, successfully creating a positive image for the community.

Halifax Regional Library (Dartmouth, Nova Scotia, Canada), http://www.halifaxpubliclibraries.ca/
Annotation from LAMA: Halifax Regional Library, Dartmouth, Nova Scotia, Canada, for its re-designed Summer Reading Program. With a skateboarding dog, Booker T. Beagle, and animal "Book Buddies" for younger children, the program creatively used a consistent graphic identity, a dynamic Web site, and targeted marketing to reach the intended audience.

Julia Rogers Library, Goucher College (Baltimore, MD), http://www. goucher.edu/x643.xml
Annotation from LAMA: Julia Rogers Library, Goucher College, Baltimore, Md., for the public relations program "25 Years of Jane Austen," designed to bring increased attention to this unique collection. The identification of strategies for the campaign, along with target audiences, was precise and comprehensive, ranging from a resident scholarship to digitizing the collection for access by a worldwide audience.

Las Vegas-Clark County Library District (Las Vegas, NV), http://www. lvccld.org/index.cfm

Annotation from LAMA: Las Vegas-Clark County Library District, Las Vegas, Nev., for its outstanding public relations campaign celebrating Asian Pacific American Heritage Month. Part of the library district's "Celebrate Cultural Diversity" initiative, the event attracted more than 6,000 people and generated positive media coverage.

Library System of Lancaster County (PA), http://www. lancasterlibraries.org/lslc/site/default.asp

Annotation from LAMA: Library System of Lancaster County, Pa., for its stimulating public awareness campaign promoting the Pennsylvania online world of electronic resources (POWER), which successfully enhanced local resources

Saint Paul (MN) Public Library and the Friends of the Saint Paul Public Library (St. Paul, MN), http://www.thefriends.org

Saint Paul (MN) Public Library and the Friends of the Saint Paul Public Library for a multi-faceted public awareness campaign to celebrate the re-opening of their newly renovated historic Central Library.

Sarasota County Library System (Sarasota, FL), http://suncat.co. sarasota.fl.us/Default.aspx

Annotation from LAMA: Sarasota County Library System, Sarasota, Fla., for its successful program "Celebrate Freedom @ Your Library™," which refocused public attention on how libraries contribute to a free society. This program, developed in answer to the challenges posed by 9/11, helped to erase the doubts raised by that tragic event that were aimed at the very core of what libraries stand for—freedom of information and access for all.

Toronto Public Library (Toronto, Canada), http://www.torontopubliclibrary. ca/index.jsp

Annotation from LAMA: Toronto Public Library, Toronto, Canada, for an innovative performing arts lecture series and public relations program that contributed to the city's literary and cultural life while also enhancing the library's community profile.

2002 Winners

Baltimore County Public Library (Towson, MD), http://www.bcplonline.org/

Annotation from LAMA: Baltimore County (Maryland) Public Library, for its innovative program "Baby Boosters," promoting the library as an important resource for parents and caregivers of preschoolers. The program used volunteers, colorful posters, and a dynamic Web page to attract its target audience.

Bowling Green Public Library (Bowling Green, KY), http://www.bgpl.org/

Annotation from LAMA: Bowling Green (Kentucky) Public Library, for a campaign to turn a historic railroad depot into a branch library, featuring a technology hub and an early childhood center. The focus is on services to young children, parents, and caregivers.

Calgary Public Library (Alberta, Canada), http://calgarypubliclibrary.com/

Annotation from LAMA: Calgary Public Library (Alberta, Canada), for its television campaign "Rediscover Your Calgary Library." Vibrant spots highlighting library resources stressed the value and convenience of library services.

Maryland State Department of Education, Division of Library Development Services (Baltimore, MD), http://www.marylandpublicschools.org/msde/divisions/library

Annotation from LAMA: Maryland State Department of Education, Division of Library Development Services, for the campaign "It's Never Too Early." This statewide initiative promotes reading by connecting parents and caregivers of preschool children with local public library services.

New York Public Library (New York, NY), http://www.nypl.org/

Annotation from LAMA: New York Public Library, for "Where the Performing Arts Live." This plan raised the curtain on a $37 million, three-year renovation project for one of the city's most valuable resources—The New York Public Library's performing arts collections.

Appendix D

Sample Marketing Plans

Avon Grove Library Marketing Campaign

Submitted by Kim Ringler

An Early Literacy Program for Babies and Their Parents

Part 1: Executive summary

Mission Statement

The Avon Grove Library provides materials, services, and programming designed to meet the diverse educational, recreational, and cultural needs of the community. It supports universal access to information, inspires the love of reading, and promotes literacy and lifelong learning.

Purpose of This Marketing Plan

The library will implement a new parent-infant program entitled: *Be with Me –Read with Me,* in the fall of 2005. This offering, which is designed to support social interaction, reading development, and community collaboration, will begin with a public information session, a kick-off breakfast, and the initiation of the first six-week session. In addition, new children's board book collections will be made available through the baby "*Be with Me* Backpack" kits. Adult parenting books on early literacy will also be displayed. An informational resource package, which contains related brochures, will also be distributed. This plan endeavors to outline the basic goals, objectives, and strategies needed to carry out and bring awareness to the program and corresponding events, as well as promote the services and materials associated with the general operations of the library.

Executive Summary

In the fall of 2004, the Avon Grove Library received a grant from a private corporation to implement an early literacy program for babies and their parents. Working on the tenets of several recognized training programs in the field, these sessions are designed not only to engage the child, but also to provide greater opportunities for parents to learn about their child's intellectual development. These interactive programs will be given predominately by library staff. One session per six-week offering will feature a presentation by a visiting outside early childhood professional. The program, which is designed for children ages birth to 2 and their parents, incorporates simple stories, songs, rhymes, finger plays, baby games, and age-appropriate crafts. Each session will be one hour long, and will accommodate 18 families. Avon Grove Library will host two separate but consecutive sessions per week. All sessions are free to the public.

In preparation, the library first conducted a community needs assessment directed toward parents with very young children. This allowed the library administration to formulate goals that specifically addressed the needs of the community. Results of this survey indicated that there was sufficient interest to host a separate bilingual *Be with Me—Read with Me* session that would also address the needs of the Hispanic community. This factor caused a bifurcation in the target population, a situation that also channels the marketing endeavors in two directions.

The overall goals for this program include:

➢ To create and promote a high-quality early literacy program.

➢ To create a sufficient staff to run the program. Also, to create an informed staff.

➢ To increase the circulation of board books and parenting books available in both English and Spanish.

➢ Increase library attendance and card registrations.

➢ Promote the overall services and materials of the library.

➢ Increase community collaborations.

The program will begin with a special kick-off breakfast, orientation, and tour of the library. Marketing endeavors will be supported by promotional items, including posters, bookmarks, fact sheets, flyers and newsletters. Radio announcements and press releases will also be an important component. Creative packaging and displays will assist with the marketing of the special collections ascribed to this offering. Since this program is dynamic in nature, marketing endeavors will be recurrent.

Part II: Current Situation & Market Research

A. Demographics & Background

The Avon Grove Library, established in 1874, is located in the heart of West Grove Borough, and is situated in a rural section of Southern Chester County, Pennsylvania. Presently, the service population is approximately 25,000. Patrons are drawn from a rich cross-section of economic levels, ethnic groups and, age ranges.

According to the Chester County Planning Commission's population projections, Chester County should have experienced a total population increase of 6% from 2000 to 2005. The population increase for those in the 0 to 4-year old range is 2%. Based on this, it is estimated that there are approximately 1,900 children under the age of four residing in this service area. Since our efforts are directed at parents with children birth to 2 years of age, this figure is important.

Based on the 2000 United States Census, other demographic characteristics for this area include:

➢ 9% of the total population in this service area are Hispanic.

➢ 17% of the population of West Grove Borough is Hispanic.

➢ Less than 2% of the population is from other ethnic or minority groups.

➢ The average annual median income for the entire area is $69,729.

➢ 83.4% of this population is classified as a high school graduate or higher

Census statistics pertaining to the Hispanic population may not be entirely accurate, as many have non-citizen status. A large number of mushroom industries are located in this region, entities that have become common places of employment for the Hispanic agricultural worker.

Similarly, economic and educational limitations for local Hispanics are evident. For example, according to statistics gathered by the Chester County Even Start Education Office, 40 percent of Hispanics employed in southern Chester County have low literacy rates in their native language. At least 75 percent of these have limited or no English language proficiency. In addition, the vast majorities of these individuals are considered low-income and require assistance for basic needs. The average annual income of a mushroom worker is $16,500, a minuscule amount when compared to the median average family income reflected in the census.

B. Needs Assessment

In February of 2005, a community survey was made available to the public. It specifically addressed the needs of individuals who have young children. To accommodate one of the potential target markets, surveys were also available in Spanish. Results indicated that there was sufficient interest from the Hispanic community to warrant a separate bilingual offering. Other things gained from this survey indicated that: A) morning hours are preferred, B) educational development was a top area of interest, and C) the majority of surveys came from residents of West Grove Borough, London Grove Township, and New London Township. Additional information rendered in these surveys will also be used in the future to formulate new family-oriented or children's programs.

C. Staff & Environment

Currently, there are eighteen staff members employed at the library. The administration, including Director, Kim Ringler; Assistant Director, Alisa Pito; as well as Marketing Coordinator, Karen Olson, will oversee the marketing and grant administration, along with evaluation procedures. Children's department professionals, Carole Vinciguerra, Marina VanRenssen, and Denise Thomson, will implement the actual program.

Part III: Product Overview

Products:

➢ The "Be with Me—Read with Me" early literacy program
Purpose: To provide a quality program for babies and their parents by using trained staff and one visiting outside professional per 6-week session.

➢ The "Be with Me—Read with Me" baby backpacks & parenting books
Purpose: To provide a convenient method of packaging books to encourage reading everyday, while simultaneously improving circulation.

➢ The "kick-off" breakfast, open house, and library tour
Purpose: To provide a relaxed environment to initiate the program, and to provide an introduction to other library materials and services.

Pricing: This is free to all registrants, a factor that keeps the library competitive.

Distribution Channels: Marketing promotional items will be distributed through the library, elementary schools, daycares, area businesses, and supporting agencies, including the Southern Chester County Literacy Coalition, and Catholic Social Services. Press releases and a radio spot are also incorporated. A posting will be placed on the library's home page via the event keeper program. Direct mailing of invitations is also planned.

Part IV: Target Population

Based on the results of the needs assessment conducted in February, two potential target markets exist. The plan must address the fact that it is marketing to both the child and the parent of each group. They are:

➢ Segment # 1: Babies and toddlers, ages birth–2, with parents who speak only Spanish

➢ Segment # 1 (a): Babies and toddlers, ages birth–2, with parents who are bilingual

➢ Segment # 2: Babies and toddlers, ages birth–2, with parents who speak English

All of the above groups will be influenced by time, price, location, and educational value. Those that speak only Spanish may be influenced by social and language accommodation. From past experience, it has been found that those new to this county, especially if they speak limited English, tend to participate in activities where there is a predominate number of other people in the same cultural and language group. With this in mind, it was decided that one of the sessions should be directed toward the Hispanic population, including those with limited English language skills. Means and distribution will vary for each market segment.

Part V: Goals & Objectives

Goal 1: To create and promote a high-quality early literacy program that meets the needs of children, ages birth to 2, and their parents or caregivers.

Objective 1:1—Between May and September of 2005, have ready for distribution the following promotional/advertising items: press releases, sign-up sheets, bookmarks, flyers, invitations and signage.

Objective 1:2—By June of 2005, prepare the children's room to accommodate the extra equipment and supplies needed for this program.

Objective 1:3—By July of 2005, purchase and display posters, banners, etc. to place in the children's room.

Objective 1:4—On September 16, 2005, hold a kick-off breakfast for all registrants. Invitations will be sent out by September 5, 2005.

Objective 1:5—By September of 2005, implement a program, entitled: Be with Me—Read with Me," based on rotating themes.

Goal 2: To create sufficient children's staff to run the program. Also, to create an informed library staff.

Objective 2:1—By July of 2005, provide basic training to the children's staff via a series of formal and informal workshops.

Objective 2:2—By August of 2005, inform all library staff concerning the basic elements and procedures relevant to this program, along with any promotional items distributed. In addition, schedule ongoing bi-weekly staff meetings.

Objective 2:3—Hire a bilingual children's assistant to work with the English and Spanish groups for this program.

Goal 3: To increase the circulation of juvenile board books and adult parenting books in both English and Spanish.

Objective 3:1—By June 1, 2005, purchase $2,000.00 in new board books (English & bilingual versions).

Objective 3:2—By June 1, 2005, purchase $3,000.00 in adult parenting books (English & Spanish).

Objective 3:3—By August 1, 2005, have the "Be with Me" baby backpacks processed and filled with the selected new board books. Display these prior to the opening session.

Objective 3:4—By September 15, 2005, have all adult parenting books on display.

Objective 3:5—By November of 2005, circulation of board books in English will increase by 2%.

Objective 3:6—By November of 2005, circulation of board books in Spanish will increase by 2%.

Objective 3:3—By November of 2005, circulation of new parenting books in English will increase by 1%.

Objective 3:4—By November of 2005, circulation of new parenting books in Spanish will increase by 1%.

Goal 4: To increase attendance and card registrations.

Objective 4:1—From September to November, attendance for children's programming will increase 4% per month.

Objective 4:2—Attendance for each session will be no less than 80%.

Objective 4:3—As a result of this program, new patron registration will increase by 20 for each 6-week session.

Goal 5: To promote overall services and materials of the library.

Objective 5:1—On September 16, 2005, 100 percent of all registrants will be given a tour of the facility and given information about the library and its services to the community.

Objective 5:2—General circulation, computer use, and regular story time attendance will increase by 2% per month.

Objective 5:3—From September to November, at least two individuals attending the bilingual early literacy program will join the adult literacy class.

Goal 6: To increase community collaborations.

Objective 6:1—The library will partner with at least one English-speaking early literacy professional per 6-week session.

Objective 6:2—The library will partner with at least one bilingual early literacy professional per 6-week session.

Objective 6:3—The library will partner with at least two agencies to help distribute the planned promotional items.

Objective 6:4—The library will make contact with at least three newspapers to ensure press coverage.

Part VI: Budget

Expenditures for a Two-Year Period:

Category	Programming Grant	Library Contribution	Total Cost
Personnel			
Training—Children's staff members	$5,000.00		$5,000.00
Regular staff salaries (this program only)		$5,000.00	$5,000.00
Bilingual staff Assistant (this program only)	$1,600.00		$1,600.00
Volunteers (in-kind donation)	N/A	N/A	N/A
Publicity			

Graphics/Promotional Materials (posters, bookmarks, newsletters, flyers, banner, etc.)	$4,000.00		$4,000.00
Advertising	$200.00		$200.00
Supplies			
Baby Backpacks	$800.00		$800.00
Furnishings & Equipment			
Storage cabinet	$600.00		$600.00
CD player, musical instruments, and other related items	$400.00		$400.00
Other			
Special events—refreshments	$600.00		$600.00
Books			
Board Books—English	$500.00	$500.00	$1,000.00
Board Books—Bilingual	$500.00	$500.00	$1,000.00
Adult Parenting Books—English		$1,500.00	$1,500.00
Adult Parenting Books—Spanish		$1,500.00	$1,500.00
English and Spanish educational brochures	$800.00		$800.00
TOTALS	**$15,000.00**	$9,000.00	**$24,000.00**

Income for a Two-Year Period:

Source	Amount
Corporate Programming Grant	$15,000.00
Collection Development Grant	$4,000.00
Library Operations	$5,000.00
TOTAL	$24,000.00

Part VII: Evaluation

In order to evaluate the overall program, several measurement techniques, both quantitative and qualitative in nature, will be employed to determine the fulfillment of the stated marketing/program goals and objectives. The methodology will formative in nature, with evaluation completed at intervals. That is, each six-week session will be evaluated separately. Modifications will be made as needed. At the end of the two-year funding period, a final summative evaluation will occur. The expected outcomes for each of the goals and objectives will be used as points for evaluation.

The evaluation team, which is comprised of at least two members from collaborating agencies and the children's staff from the library, will develop evaluation criteria. The Children's Librarian will issue a written evaluation, including recommendations for improvement or modification, to the Library Director. These evaluation reports will be issued at the end of each six-week period. At the end of the two-year grant period, the Library Director will compile a summary evaluation. Upon approval of all committee members, a final report will be issued.

The information derived from this evaluation will be used to modify or improve the program. The analysis of strengths and weaknesses, based on the program summary report, will become the basis for making recommendations concerning future programming.

Evaluation results will be reported to all stakeholders including: the Library Board of Trustees, all collaborating agencies, and all grantors. Results will also be made available to the public via newsletters or annual reports.

Scott Township Public Library

Submitted by Janet Forton

Scott Township Public Library recently celebrated its fifth anniversary. To celebrate, and to market the library's services, the library organized a celebration event.

Before it could create a market plan for this celebration, the library staff members had to a SWOT analysis of their community. Here's what they discovered:

Summary of External Environmental Factors

External Environmental Factors

The 2000 US Census indicates that Scott Township has 17,288 residents. However, the township appears to be losing population. According to the 2004 US Census Fact Finder, the population has decreased to 16,550. Scott Township is comprised predominately by "White Non-Hispanic". Its ancestral lines are predominately German, Italian and Irish, at almost 20% for each.

Regarding education levels of the adult population, almost 90% have achieved high school level or above. Thirty-five percent have a bachelors degree or higher. The township is within the Chartiers Valley School District. This district educates 3,400 students from Scott and the other communities Chartiers Valley serves. However, a majority of the students come from Scott Township. There are over 200 employees at the School District, which is the largest employer in the community.

Over half the population is married. Just over 20% have never married and 10% are widowed. Twenty-one percent of the population is over 65. Of the total population just over 60% are in the labor force. Two-hundred and five families (4.5%) were below poverty status in 1999.

The township covers a hilly area of almost 4 sq miles. It is a suburban community, with no center of town and no center of industry or business. There are several shopping strip malls. The townships businesses are mainly involved in the service industry. Wal*Mart moved into the community 3 years ago. Lowes will be coming soon as will some new Walgreen stores. Many of the smaller stores are owned and operated by local residents.

The township has a majority of registered Democrats. There are now 9 commissioners and a township manager.

There are numerous churches with active congregations. Two of the Catholic Churches offer K-8th grade parochial education. There are several Jewish Temples and the Jewish Community Center. Generally, the community is conservative and hardworking.

There are several local community groups. They include: The Scott Conservancy, several historical buildings: Neville House and Old St. Luke's. Summer Baseball season is very popular, as is attendance at the local community pool. The Township also sponsors annually a 4th of July celebration and an October Fest.

Seven of the eight surrounding communities have larger populations. Six have their own libraries.

EXTERNAL SWOT:

Strength:
- Relationship with Scott Conservancy already.
- Promote Old St. Luke Church.

Weakness:
- Losing population.
- Almost ¼ of the population is considered senior.
- Lack of relationship with school district.
- No association with Neville House.
- Minimal connection with the churches.
- Minimal connections with the schools (public & private).
- Minimal connections with local businesses.
- Because this library is only 5 years, people established relationships with other libraries.
- Bond locks in the % of taxes the library can ever receive.

Opportunity:
- "Center" of town.
- Build relations with the Commissioners.
- PALS program with JCC (Jewish Community Center).
- Offer programs at the pool and advertise at baseball games.
- Build relationships with new businesses moving into the community.
- Connect with the two communities that do not have their own libraries.
- Offer services for job hunting.

Threat:
- At least six other libraries are close to the boarders of the community.
- Local amusement and entertainment centers and businesses.
- Some of the commissioners don't have library cards, possibly indicating they are not support-ers of the library.

Internal Environmental Factors

STPL's Mission Statement: *The mission of the Scott Township Public Library is to provide the community with a center for reading, research and learning.*

STPL Goals

- Ensure access to current, quality reading material and research by all members of the community by acquiring, organizing and administering a quality collection of books, journals and other material of cultural, educational, informational and recreational value
- Increase reading interest among citizens, especially our youth
- Provide an important amenity to residents and potential residents
- Promote a convenient area for research and study
- Provide quality programs that seek to enrich the community and the lives of its citizens
- Cooperate with area schools and community groups in promoting library use and encouraging reading and study
- Participate in the state, regional and district library systems

At this time there are no specific written objectives to support these goals.

The board of Directors and the Staff of the library are re-examining the mission and goals and will be writing the objectives to support the goal.

Resources

- Human:
  - Staff: 3 full-time; 4 part-time (1 L of A). 2 MLIS graduates; 1 MIS graduate; 2 MLIS in-work.
  - Board: 6 Members
  - Shared Service: 1 part time cataloguer
  - Volunteers: 25 active, reliable, well trained volunteers
  - FOL: Over 200 members
  - Active Teen Advisory Board (TAB)
  - Students who need to get FLEX credit are handy for special projects
- Financial
  - Over $90,000 in the bank
  - Over $20,000 invested with The Pittsburgh Foundation
  - Several on-going memorial funds
  - State possibly increase library funding
- Technical
  - Internet access
  - MS Office Products
  - 12 computers connect to the internet
  - 3 printers (1 color: Staff use only, 1 LaserJet: Staff use only, 1 Laserjet: Staff and Patron use.)
  - 2 Phone lines and one fax.
  - 1 projector to hook up to a PC to display PowerPoints and other computer based programs.
- Physical
  - 30,000+ collection size. Large movie election, especially Hindi films.
  - Nice children's "area".
    - Located in the Municipal Building with the police, tax office and other municipal offices.

- o Free parking.
- o Small (2,900 sq ft); only one office area shared by many people. Much of the library work needs to be done in the library. The acoustics are bad. There is no separate space for a children's library. In fact, the marketing and development staff member has a computer at home and works from there—since there is not enough room at the library.
- o Shared access to community and caucus rooms
- o Good location off main road, and close to the pool.

Structure

Source: The Scott Township Public Library 2005 Annual Report

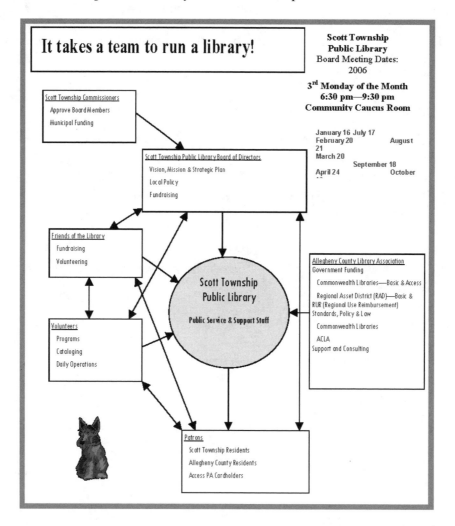

The library staff has a Director, Circulation Librarian, Director of Marketing and Development, and a Children's Librarian. The remaining are Assistant Librarians and work part-time. These staff members primary responsibilities are smooth operation of the circulation desk, assisting the patrons, and handling financial transactions. Some of the assistants have library experience, one has none.

Internal SWOT:

Strength:
- Well functioning, creative & dedicated team (staff & volunteers).
- 4 staff members live in the township.
- Volunteers!!! Many day-to-day tasks are handled by volunteers. One or two in particular are responsible for crucial aspects of library operations: Programming and Cataloging. They are both senior citizens, are very dedicated to the library.
- FOL Annual Book sale.
- FOL healthy financial situation.
- Library healthy financial situation.
- Internet access & MS Office Products.
- On a bus route.

Weakness:
- Lack of time for board members to work on mission, goals, objectives, and fundraising.
- Board is short one person & needs to recruit another one for next year that has an accounting background.
- All of the staff is underpaid and overworked. Medical benefits are offered to full-time employees. The library can help with a small portion of the monthly fee for coverage. The coverage is expensive.
- Collection needs a refresh on reference and technical materials.
- One staff member is on medical leave. This person is experienced and knowledgeable.
- Temporary replacement is "only temporary".
- Volunteers: Don't have back-ups, goals, and responsibilities and many provide critical functions.
- FOL—Lack of leadership. (Although this is changing.)
- The previous director alienated many people throughout the community.
- New director has limited public library experience.
- Will overrun budget in 2006.
- Not all staff is proficient with the computers.
- Library size—can't grow collection much more and not all staff can work at the library at the same time. (This includes volunteer catalogers.)
- Share the community room and caucus room facilities, often not available when needed or get bumped because the commissioners or police need it.
- No ultimate control over activities and programs the library can sponsor. ie. No Animals.
- No WIFI connectivity.
- Limited space for Story Times.

Opportunity:
- Hirer temporary to permanent status.
- Pursue Grants to fund special programs and projects.
- Teach staff more computer skills.
- Find a new space or build a new space.

- Demonstrate to the community that "things have changed" and that the library is a more inviting place, a place they want to be involved with.
- Work with the FOL to achieve great membership and fundraising goals.

Threat:
- Achieving proper spending and collection size development to continue to receive State, RAD and RAD-RUR funding—given the limited space to work with.
- No computer upgrades for another 2 years.
- Lack of staff time to learn new computer skills.
- Other libraries offering more programs and more convenient times and on a bigger variety of topics.
- Other libraries offering better pay and benefits.
- Strategic plan is languishing.

Once the library had information about its community, the staff could create a marketing plan for its fifth anniversary celebration. Here's the plan:

Scott Township Public Library
Marketing Plan: 5th Anniversary Celebration

Marketing Plan

Executive Summary

The marketing mission for Scott Township Public Library is to raise awareness in the community about the library and to position the library as a community center.

This project's scope is a subset of the overall marketing plan for the library. The main goal of this project is to host a 5th Anniversary Celebration which is fun, inviting and helps with our branding efforts, "see Scottie—think 'The Library!' " Many of the goals and objectives outlined in the main plan will either be accomplished via this project, or initiated with this project.

We will introduce Scottie, our mascot that day. The new mascot logo will be on the invitation and all other Scott Township Public Library information and publications. This party will be designed to appeal to young and old and everyone in between. We anticipate 25% of the people who receive invitations will attend the event. We want to send a minimum of 200 invitations to non-library patrons.

The library staff has 9 weeks to accomplish this project once the approval of the board has been received. We have a limited budget of $600 so we will be relying heavily on donations. We also need the assistance of our volunteers before and during the event.

The Director of the Library is ultimately responsible for the planning and success of this project. This will also be a good test to see how well the newly established staff of the library work together under pressure.

Project Scope

The event, or project, will last for one day. It will be on Saturday, March 25, 2006. The party will occur during regular library hours which are 9:30am—4:30 pm. The intended impact is to last well beyond the one day of official activities for the party. Many of the goals and objectives outlined in the library's Marketing Plan, and listed below will be accomplished through the activities of this project.

Marketing Plan 2006, Goals & Objectives
The items which are in bold will be accomplished via this project.
The items which are in italics will be initiated during this project.

1. *Service Goals*
   - *Communicate more effectively and on a regular basis with the community.*
   - *Attract additional "regular & reliable" volunteers in order to ease the current burden on the staff and other volunteers.*
2. *Funding Goals*
   - *Prepare the community for a Capital Campaign.*
3. *Positioning/Promotion goals*
   - **"A cozy place to be."**
   - Inviting place, all are welcome here!
   - Scottie Mascot/see the logo and think "The Library!"
   - **Promote National Library Week.**
   - **Promote Summer Reading Program.**
   - Promote weekly Children's Story Time and bi-monthly Baby Lapsit.
   - **Promote Friends of the Library.**
   - **Promote the need for Volunteers.**

4. *Facilities goals*
    - **Facilitate knowing where to find "things"—A map of the library.**
5. *Customer goals*
    - *Increase number and variety of programs and attendance at the programs.*
    - Bring back alienated community members.
6. *New product/service goals*
    - **Community Information Service.**
    - Kiosk—for information display.
    - *Increased media exposure.*
    - **5 years and going strong!**
    - **Introduce Celtic collection (new anonymous donation).**

Key areas to focus on:

1. **Media Contacts**: Establish contacts. Learn time frames and format for press releases.
2. **School (public and private) Contacts:** Begin to open the doors of communication. Let them know that we are here. Learn how to best communicate with the different groups.
3. **Elected Official:** Establish communication channels with them. Remind them that the library provides a "value added" service to the community. Look for additional ways to be of service to their particular needs.
4. **Branding, "See Scottie, think 'The Library' ":** Develop the Scottie Dog as our brand. In part to play on the new Celtic collection and to tie with the township name. Make Scottie "cute enough" to appeal to the young, and sophisticated enough to be on official documents, letter head, etc.
5. **Re-Invigorate the community:** Help get the word out that many changes, for the good, have occurred at their library. Children's area is spruced up. Collection is cleaned up. New things are happening—come back and join us.
6. **Have fun:** If we don't have fun hosting the party—then why do it at all? People will sense that we love what we are doing and will want to join us.

Roles & Responsibilities

Board of Directors: Approval of the project. Support the project.

Library Director: Develop the marketing plan and support the initiatives stemming from the plan. Find additional resources, including revenue to implement this project. The director is also responsible for the positive outcome of the party.

Marketing and Development Director: Participate in developing the marketing plan. Develop list of community connections, media, schools, churches and other business and service organizations within the township. Develop a working relationship with the Commissioners. Develop the Community Information Service initiative.

Library Staff: Provide input into the marketing plan. Participate in the many tasks to accomplish the 5th Anniversary party.

FOL: Continue to support the library with fundraising events. Help with the project.

Volunteers: Help prepare for the party. Help the day of the party.

The Project Plan & Budget

	Task	Who	Due Date	Notes	
A.	Secure Facilities	A.	2/14/06	Conference room, hall way & outside if possible.	
B.	Invitations	A.	2/25/06	Mail 'em!	247.00
C.	Publicity	B.	3/18/06	The bulk of the contacts finished. Follow up the week before.	
D.	Library Ready?	A.	3/24/2006	Friday	40.00
E.	Working that day?	Everyone!	3/25/2006	Saturday!	
F.	Food	C.	3/24/2006	Friday	52.00
G.	Tables	A.	3/22/2006	Where, and for what.	38.00
H.	Capture the Day	A.	3/22/2006	Photos? Video?	
I.	Entertainment	B.	3/22/2006	Music, Food and Fun!	100.00
J.	History of Library	B.	3/22/2006	It took almost 40 years to get the library. Who & how.	
K.	Copies Made	A.	3/23/2006	Get the information in the patron's hands. Communicate!	18.00
L.	Guest Book & Flip Charts	A.	3/22/06	Invite people to be a part of the party immediately. Tie into National Library Week. Communicate activities.	8.00
M.	Donation "Dog House"	D.	3/24/06	Donations (Financial & supplies). Communicate that we need them. Stick to our dog theme.	8.00
N.	Chinese Auction	E.	3/24/06	Fundraiser. A way to involve the local businesses via donations.	
O.	Children's Time 2-4	F.	3/25/06	But all crafts ready by Wednesday, 3/22/06	15.00
P.	Vendors	B.	3/20/06	Supply a variety of items, while not detracting from raising funds for us. Make sure to not overlap in sales items.	
Q.	Scottie Promotional Items	B.	3/22/06	T-Shirts and Totes to sell. See what the traffic will bear.	35.00
R.	Scottie Mascot Outfit	A.	3/23/06	Really get our "brand" out there.	
S.	Street Sign	A.	3/22/06	Vote Sign decorated for Greentree & Lindsay	
T.	Clean-up & Follow-up	A.	4/15/06	All thank-you notes out by 4/15/06.	6.00
Estimated Total Expenses:					**567.00**

Detail Project Plan

	Task	Who	Due Date or Status	Notes		
A.	**Secure Facilities**	A.	**14-Feb-06**			
A. 1	Conference Room	A.	Complete	Reserve via FF.		
A. 2	Halls OK to use?	A.	Complete	Check with GG. and HH.		
A. 3	Animals OK?	A.	Complete	NO :{ Township has liability concerns.		
B.	**Invitations**	A.	**25-Feb-06**			
B. 1	*The Invitation*					
B. 2	Paper	A.	Complete	Not card stock, but heavier white paper.	22.00	
B. 3	Envelopes	A.	Complete	Invitation size 8 ½ x 5	55.00	
B. 4	Stamps	A.	Complete	Resolved send as many as possible.	170.00	
B. 5	Design	A.	Complete	Multiple ones created by 2/23/06. Then work with the staff to pick/refine one.		
B. 6	*Contact Lists*		**25-Feb-06**			
B. 7	Order Labels	A.	Complete	Can use the rest for regular office supplies.		
B. 8	Make Labels	A.	Complete	For all—unless CC. decides to do her own.		
B. 9	FOL	A.	Complete	Check for accuracy and update.		
B. 10	Volunteers	A.	Complete	Check for accuracy and update.		
B. 11	Scott Township Workers	A.	Complete	Hand deliver: Police, Tax Office, Magistrate, etc.		
B. 12	Other Libraries	A.	Complete	Assemble and send via ILL process.		
B. 13	ACLA	A.	Complete	Assemble and send via ILL process.		
B. 14	eiNetwork	A.	Complete	Assemble and send via ILL process.		
B. 15	Legislators	B.	Complete	Mail and phone call follow up.		
B. 16	Previous Speakers	B.	Complete	Work with H. to ID list.		

Detail Project Plan (*Cont.*)

	Task	Who	Due Date or Status	Notes	
B. 17	CV School District	A.	Complete	Assemble and have kids deliver to offices.	
B. 18	Local Businesses	B.	Complete	Hand deliver with posters to hang.	
B. 19	Churches & JCC	B.	Complete	Mail and/or hand deliver. (Learned the church and the schools don't communicate. Need to invite each separately.)	
C.	**Publicity**	**B.**	**3/17/06**	**All contacts made once by week before.**	
C. 1	II.	B.	Complete	WYEP Broadcast? "Echoes of Erin"	
C. 2	Gateway Papers	B.	Complete	They want to come and take pictures.	
C. 3	Almanac	B.	Complete	Contact Made/Writing Article	
C. 4	Post Gazette	B.	Complete	Press Release Sent, follow-up phone call	
C. 5	Tribune	B.	Complete	Press Release Sent, follow-up phone call	
C. 6	KDKA	B.	Complete	Camera Crews? (And Dave Crawley if possible.)	
C. 7	WTAE	B.	Complete	Camera Crews?	
C. 8	WPXI	B.	Complete	Camera Crews?	
C. 9	FOX	B.	Complete	Camera Crews?	
C. 10	Posters—Make/assemble	B. & SD	3/14/06 Complete	Use the invitation and set up on poster paper.	
C. 11	Posters—Distribute	B. & SD	3/14/06 Complete	Take to businesses in the community for display.	
C. 12	Update our Website	A.	On-Hold	Art Institute Students will Update in April/May.	
C. 13	CIS Form On website	A.	On-Hold	Art Institute Students will Update in April/May.	
D.	**Library Ready?**	**A.**	**3/24/2006**	**Friday**	
D. 1	K. Plotts—Special Cleaning	A.	3/17/06 Complete	Rugs & Chairs & Windows—above and beyond normal cleaning. Communicate with K.	40.00

Detail Project Plan (*Cont.*)

	Task	Who	Due Date or Status	Notes		
D. 2	Move Reference	A.	3/24/06 Complete	So "map of library" can be made and distributed. A., F., O., V., N., B., D. & DD. do all the moves.		
D. 3	Move YA & J	A.	3/24/06 Complete	So "map of library" can be made and distributed. & A., F., O., V., N., B., D. & DD. do all the moves.		
D. 4	Move all Non-Fiction & Bibliographies, Audio Books, some DVDs and Paperbacks.	A.	3/24/06 Complete	So "map of library" can be made and distributed. & A., F., O., V., N., B., D. & DD. do all the moves.		
D. 5	Cover back of Xerox	A.	Cancelled	Turn so the back faces the wall.		
D. 6	Hang all new signs	A.	In-Work	To facilitate finding items, especially with all the moves outlined above.		
D. 7	Make New sign for Bricks	A.	On-Hold	Just not enough time		
D. 8	Hang New Brick Sign	A.	On-Hold			
D. 9	Receive donated Celtic Collection	A.	1/31/06	How neat is that?!		
D. 10	Catalog new items	G.	3/17/06	Decide categories, shelving, display etc. and complete as many as possible a week before the party.		
D. 11	Process items	Volunteers	3/22/06	Covers, spine labels, book plates installed.		
D. 12	Released to the collection	C.	3/24/06	Set status to Available and place Neon Green label on spine.		
D. 13	Celtic Display Set-up	A.	Complete	Decide where to display for the party. And set it up!		
D. 14	Clean up Office area	A.	3/24/06 Complete	Make sure there is enough room for volunteers to store coats, hand bags. Secure everything.		
D. 15	Clean up Kitchen area	A.	3/24/06 Complete	Make sure there is enough room to stage food and drinks for party.		
D. 16	Donated books across the street	A.	3/24/06 Complete	Clear the area by the Circulation Desk.		

Detail Project Plan (*Cont.*)

	Task	Who	Due Date or Status	Notes					
D. 17	New Patron Applications	A.	3/23/06 Complete	Make sure enough are printed and cut.					
D. 18	FOL Membership Forms	A.	3/22/06 Complete	Update format. Prepare for copying.					
D. 19	Library Floor plan	A.	Complete	Design, print and display through out the library.					
D. 20	Welcome Brochure	C.	3/22/06 Complete	Finish the final touches so it is ready for copying.					
D. 21	I Want to Volunteer Forms	A.	3/22/06 Complete	Design and prepare for copying.					
D. 22	Advertise Funding/Budget	A.	Complete	Contact your legislators! Display letter					
D. 23	Advertise for NLW	A.	3/23/06 Complete	Design and prepare for copying.					
D. 24	Advertise for One Book	H.	Use what we have already.	One Community—One Book					
D. 25	Advertise for children's Pgms. (Book Marks)	F.	3/22/06 Complete	Story Time, Baby Lap Sit					
D. 26	Advertise for SRP	A.	3/24/06 Complete	Design and prepare for copying.					
D. 27	Community Information Service	B.	3/14/06 Complete	Design and prepare for copying. Present to commissioners on the 14th.					
E.	Working that day?	Everyone!	3/25/2006	Saturday!					
E. 1	Circ Desk	C., I. & E.		Make sure to let them hob-knob also!					
E. 2	Hob-Knobbing	A.	All Day	Prepare outfit. (Coldwater Creek!!)					
E. 3	Hob-Knobbing	B.	All Day						
E. 4	Hob-Knobbing	C.	Complete	A. assign times and duties: 8:30—10, Veggie & Fruit trays; help set-up on Saturday AM.					Donated

Detail Project Plan (*Cont.*)

	Task	Who	Due Date or Status	Notes	
E. 5	Hob-Knobbing	J.	Complete	A. assign times and duties: 9:00-11:30 Soda & ice; help set-up on Saturday AM.	Donated
E. 6	Hob-Knobbing	K.	Complete	A. assign times and duties: 9:00-11:30 Soda & ice; help set-up on Saturday AM.	Donated
E. 7	Hob-Knobbing	L.	Complete	A. assign times and duties: 1:00-3:30 Soda & ice; Make sure to meet with X.—future bookkeeper?	Donated
E. 8	Hob-Knobbing	M.	Complete	A. assign times and duties: 10:00-2:00 Soda & ice. He and his wife will also help monitor the cookie table and keep the TV/videos running.	Donated
E. 9	Hob-Knobbing	N.	Complete	A. assign times and duties: Cups & Ice. Help Friday night.	Donated
F.	**Food**	**C.**	**3/24/2006**	**Friday**	
F. 1	*Cookies*	C. G.			
F. 2	Cookie Dough	B.	Complete	From Shop 'n Save	Donated
F. 3	Cook Cookies	C. & D. & B.	Complete	Cookie cutter shapes (Bones, Paws, Scottie Dog)	Donated
F. 4	Icing	C. & D.	Complete	What colors/how set-up so it doesn't turn into a huge mess!	10.00
F. 5	*Drinks*	A.			
F. 6	Coffee	A.	3/22/06 Complete	Get coffee pot from storage. Dorothy to make.	
F. 7	Water	D.	3/25/06 Complete		Donated
F. 8	Pepsi & Diet & Ice	J.	Complete	A. assigned. Request all delivered Friday night.	Donated
F. 9	Coke & Diet & Ice	K.	Complete	A. assigned. Request all delivered Friday night.	Donated
F. 10	Root Beer & Diet & Ice	J.	Complete	A. assigned. Request all delivered Friday night.	Donated

---

Detail Project Plan (*Cont.*)

	Task	Who	Due Date or Status	Notes	
F. 11	Seven-Up & Diet& Ice	M.	Complete	A. assigned. Request all delivered Friday night.	Donated
F. 12	Coolers	O.	Complete	Will bring 2 large	
F. 13	Coolers	K. H.	Complete	Will bring 1 large	
F. 14	*Punch*	B.			
F. 15	Ginger Ale	B.	Complete	Have from "New Director" party.	
F. 16	Hawaiian Punch	B.	Complete	Have from "New Director" party.	
F. 17	Punch Ladle (s)	A.	Complete	A.'s	
F. 18	Punch Bowl (2)Large	A.	3/22/06 Complete	A.'s	
F. 19	Small Punch Bowl for Ice	B.	Complete	One used at "New Director" party. For ice.	
F. 20	*Finger Food*	*B.*			
F. 21	Veggie Trays	C. B.	Complete	A. assigned.	Donated
F. 22	Volunteer Sign-Up List Made	A.	Complete	Create and put @ Circ. Desk	
F. 23	Bring a dish?	P.	Complete	P.—Cheese and crackers	Donated
F. 24	Bring a dish?	Q.	Complete	Q.—Turkish bread	Donated
F. 25	Sarris Bones (Chocolate)	A.	Complete	Investigate cost and size. ($1—no cost break)	
F. 26	Fruit	C. B.	Complete	A. assigned.	Donated
F. 27	*Food & Drink Set-ups*	*A.*			
F. 28	Cups	A.	3/22/06 Complete	Tumblers (9 oz) for punch & 12 oz	20.00
F. 29	Cups	N.	3/24/06 Complete	16 oz glasses (Red, White & Blue)	Donated

Detail Project Plan (*Cont.*)

	Task	Who	Due Date or Status	Notes	
F. 30	Plates	A.	3/22/06 Complete	Red, White & Blue	32.00
F. 31	Napkins	A.	3/22/06 Complete	White—From Adriane A.	Donated
F. 32	Wipes for hands	D.	3/22/06 Complete	Put out by cookie table for pre & post decorating.	Donated
G.	**Tables**	A.	**3/22/2006**		
G. 1	Where?	A.	3/15/06	Design hall floor plan. Take measurements.	
G. 2	What Size?	A.	3/15/06	Based on measurements.	
G. 3	Who can bring some?	A.	YES!!	Randy—Township provide?	
G. 4	Friends of the Library & Volunteers	A.	YES!!	H.—Want one? Share with volunteers?	
G. 5	Food (In general) & Drinks	A.	Complete	1 or 2?	
G. 6	Cookies	A.	Complete	One—close to food and drink	
G. 7	Chinese Auction Display	A.	Complete	As people come in	
G. 8	Community Information Service	A.	Complete	By the bricks if possible	
G. 9	R. Butler	R.	Complete	R. will have her own table	
G. 10	Covers for each	A.	Complete	Red, White & Blue (Skirts & Covers)	38.00
G. 11	Tax Table (Clear off for the day?)	A.	Complete	Move to in front of tax office.	
H.	**Capture the Day**	A.	**3/22/2006**		
H. 1	Digital Camera	A.	Use A.'s & CC.'s Brothers	M.? Or Elaine in memory of Ellen S.?	

Detail Project Plan (*Cont.*)

	Task	Who	Due Date or Status	Notes	
H. 2	Photo Printer? Or	A.	Print @ Mal*Wart	Depends on if camera is donated.	
H. 3	HP 2600n for Scottie Photos?	A.	Cancelled	Not enough time to train. Too far to easily coordinate.	
H. 4	Prepare "Cards" with color in Scottie	A.	Cancelled	See above.	
H. 5	Order Ink for HP 2600n	A.	Complete	Will need for future office work. Can apply to general office supplies not specific to the party. ($400)	
I.	Entertainment	B.	*3/22/2006*		
I. 1	Face Painter?	B.	No go	Can't find anyone that is available that day.	
I. 2	Juggler?	H.	No go	E. felt it was too expensive @ $70 and couldn't convince him to do it for free.	
I. 3	Other activities	B.	Complete	Arranged for Police Fingerprinting/ID of Kids	
I. 4	*Music*				
I. 5	CD Player	B.	Complete	CC. to bring in her own and use STPLs.	
I. 6	CDs	B. & JB	Complete	Bring from personal collections to supplement libraries.	
I. 7	Bag Pipers	B. & E.	3/24/06	2:15 pm	Donated Time
I. 8	*Dancers*				
I. 9	Platform Specs	B. & O.	3/2/06 Complete	10 x 10—low to the grown. To protect floor from shoes.	
I. 10	Platform Materials	O.	3/3/06 Complete	Home Depot—again!	100.00
I. 11	Platform	O.	3/11/06 Complete	Design and build. Mark all pieces. Pre-drill, etc.	

Detail Project Plan (*Cont.*)

	Task	Who	Due Date or Status	Notes	
I. 12	Set-up Platform	O.	3/24/2006 Complete	N. & V. help	
I. 13	Irish Step Dancers	B.	2/24/06 Complete	1-1:30	Donated Time
I. 14	Caleigh Dancers	B.	2/24/06 Complete	3—3:45	Donated Time
J.	**History of Library**	**B.**	**3/22/2006**	**Wednesday**	
J. 1	Obtain information from Dorothy	B.	3/3/06	Transfer files, papers, etc.	
J. 2	Read through	B.	In-Work	Will have to finish after the party. Too much to work through to do a good job in the time available.	
J. 3	Create story layout	B.	On-Hold		
J. 4	Create document	B.	On-Hold		
K.	**Copies Made**	**A.**	**3/23/2006**	**Thursday**	
K. 1	Annual Report	A.	3/22/06 Complete	White paper; 25 copies (8 pages)	
K. 2	History	A.	Need by 3-24-06	B. needs to provide.	
K. 3	New Member applications	A.	3/22/06 Complete	White card stock; 100 copies (2 per page, 1 cut)	
K. 4	FOL Membership Forms	A.	3/22/06 Complete	Yellow paper; 100 copies (2 per page, 1 cut)	
K. 5	Library Floor plan	A.	3/24/06 Complete	White paper; 20 copies (1 per page) (And send in FOL Spring Newsletter.)	
K. 6	Welcome Brochure	C.	3/22/06 Complete	Blue paper; 100 copies (2 sided, three folds)	10.00

Detail Project Plan (*Cont.*)

	Task	Who	Due Date or Status	Notes	
K. 7	I Want to Volunteer Forms	A.	3/22/06 Complete	Violet paper; 50 copies (2 sided, three folds)	8.00
K. 8	Community Information Service	A.	3/22/06 Complete	White paper, 50 copies (1 per page.)	
L.	**Guest Book & Flip Charts**	A.			
L. 1	Purchase	A.	3/22/06	Journal type	8.00
L. 2	Set-up	A.	3/24/06 Complete	In front hall window. Create cover design.	
L. 3	Tell your Story	A.	3/25/06 Complete	Make a sign with instructions on poster board. (Write up and Elaine P. will make the sign.)	
L. 4	Flip Chart—Welcome/Orientation	A.	3/24/06 Complete	Use STPLs flip chart stand	
L. 5	Flip Chart—Activities Schedule	A.	3/24/06 Complete	Bring in A.'s flip chart stand	
M.	**Donation "Dog House"**	**D. & A.**			
M. 1	Die Cut Scottie Dogs—Order	A.	Complete		
M. 2	Dog House	D.	3/24/06 Complete	Design and do it!	
M. 3	Dog Bones	D.	3/24/06 Complete	Cut out and label with items needed.	
M. 4	Dogs	A.	3/21/06 Complete	D. to teach A. how to use die-cutter. Get silver & gold pens to write on black dogs.	8.00
M. 5	Items to request on Bones. Assemble "The Wish List"	F. & H.	2/28/06 Complete	Gift Cards: Unique Boutique, Jo Ann's; Dollar Tree; Michael's; Home Depot, sequins, feathers, etc.	
N.	**Chinese Auction**	E.			

Detail Project Plan (*Cont.*)

	Task	Who	Due Date or Status	Notes	
N. 1	Raffle Tickets	A.	3/22/06 Complete	3—Double Roll Tickets	12.00
N. 2	*Baskets*				
N. 3	**Adult**	S.	3/24/06 Complete	Assemble and Wrap	
N. 4	Items for Baskets	B.	3/24/06 Complete	Get Donations	Donated
N. 5	**Child**	E.	3/24/06 Complete	Assemble and Wrap	
N. 6	Items for Baskets	B.	3/24/06 Complete	Get Donations	Donated
N. 7	**Dog (D.)**	D.	3/24/06 Complete	Assemble and Wrap	
N. 8	Items for Baskets	B. & D.	3/24/06 Complete	Get Donations	Donated
N. 9	*Other Items to Raffle/auction:*				
N. 10	Poster of Irish Cottages	B.	Complete	Donated (But I want to hang it in the library!)	Donated
N. 11	*Process for the day*				
N. 12	Determine Price of tickets	STPL Team	3/10/06	2 for $1.00	
N. 13	Where to put money?	A.	3/10/06	Use cash box that we no longer use to collect fines.	
N. 14	Sell tickets	T.		12-4	
N. 15	Sell tickets	Staff		9:30—4	
N. 16	Sell tickets	Volunteers		9:30—4	

Detail Project Plan (*Cont.*)

	Task	Who	Due Date or Status	Notes							
N. 17	Conduct the drawing @ 4:00	D.									
N. 18	Call winners if not there.	I.									
O.	**Children's Time 2-4**	F.									
O. 1	*Book Marks*	*F.*									
justright O. 2	Design	F.	3/13/06	Settle on program dates and times. Incorporate Scottie Logo and colors into design.							
O. 3	Print in color	F.	3/14/06								
spalpha O. 4	Cut out	Volunteers	3/15/06								
O. 5	Laminate	A.	03/20/06 Complete								
O. 6	Cut Out & Hole Punch	A.	03/20/06 Complete								
O. 7	Cut Ribbon	A.	03/20/06 Complete								
O. 8	Assemble Ribbon	A.	03/20/06 Complete								
O. 9	*Scottie Magnet*	*F.*									
O. 10	Design	F.	3/13/06 Complete	Design and Create directions for cutting							
O. 11	Cut out black	Volunteers	Complete	Volunteers to cut out							
O. 12	Cut out Other parts	Volunteers	Complete	Volunteers to cut out							
O. 13	*Scottie Finger Puppet*	*F.*									
O. 14	Design	F.	3/13/06 Complete	Design.							

Detail Project Plan (*Cont.*)

	Task	Who	Due Date or Status	Notes	
O.15	Print	F.	Complete	Color in if necessary	
O.16	Cut out	Volunteers	Complete	Volunteers to cut out	
O.17	*Paper Bag Puppet*	*F.*			
O.18	Design	F.	3/13/06 Complete	Design and Create directions for cutting	
O.19	Cut out brown legs	Volunteers	Complete	Volunteers to cut out	
O.20	Cut out tail	Volunteers	Complete	Volunteers to cut out	
O.21	Cut out face parts	Volunteers	Complete	Volunteers to cut out	
O.22	Cut out yarn strips and ribbon	Volunteers	Complete	Volunteers to cut out	
O.23	*Process for the day*	*F.*			
O.24	Helper?	U.	Complete	F. recruit daughter	
O.25	Helper?	V.	Complete	A. recruit daughter	
O.26	Helper?	W.	Complete	F. contact TAB—anyone of them help?	
O.27	Yarn	F.	Complete	D. had some!	Donated
O.28	Scottie Puppet—For story time intro. Order	A.	Here!	All the way from England! To be used to start story times and baby lapsits.	$15.00
O.29	*Story Teller*	*Y.*			
O.30	Stories Selected		3/13/06 Complete	G. to help.	
O.31	Props?		Complete	None Required	
O.32	*Story Teller*	*D.*			
O.33	Stories Selected		3/13/06 Complete	G. to help.	

Detail Project Plan (*Cont.*)

	Task	Who	Due Date or Status	Notes	
O. 34	Props?		Complete	None Required	
P.	**Vendors**	B.			
P. 1	R.	B.	Complete	Tours & Jewelry	
P. 2	DD.	B.	Complete	Can't come. No Animals :{	
P. 3	Other Irish Vendors	B.	Complete	Won't come; "Too Small"	
Q.	**Scottie Promotional Items**	**B.**			
Q. 1	T-Shirts	B.	Complete	2 as examples—Adult and Children	20
Q. 2	Tote Bags	B.	Complete	1 or 2 as examples	15
Q. 3	Stationary	A.	Cancelled	Tried some designs. None were appealing and other things needed to be done.	
Q. 4	Establish Price	B.	Complete	$15 for Adult, $12.50 for Child, $15 for Tote	
Q. 5	Set-up and create sign-up sheet	B.	Complete	Hang on "Bag" stand.	
R.	**Scottie Mascot Outfit**	A.			
R. 1	Ice Packs	A.	On-Hold	Design body straps to hold ice packs. Try fans first and hope for cool weather that day!	
R. 2	Better Fan?	KB	3/25/06 Complete	Radio Shack. Also include a switch.	
R. 3	Batteries for Fan	A.	3/22/06 Complete	Will need for all future visits.	
R. 4	Make Hat	A.	On-Hold	Red/blue—flannel plaid	
R. 5	Make Scarf	A.	On-Hold	Blue with Library Logo or Red with Library Logo	
R. 6	Wearing	Z.	Complete	DD. get a buddy to help. Make sure they both know that young kids (18 mos., 3 years and some 5 year-olds) are some times fearful of costumes like these and to leave them alone.	

Detail Project Plan (*Cont.*)

	Task	Who	Due Date or Status	Notes	
R. 7	Pictures with Scottie	BB.	Cancelled	BB. to just take photos of kids who were finger printed. Let Scottie roam around.	
R. 8	Print on card with color in Scottie on inside?	A.	Cancelled	Need someone to take and print. Had no time to recruit and train for this.	
S.	**Street Sign**	A.		**Greentree & Lindsay**	
S. 1	Decorate "Vote" sign	A.	3/22/06 Complete	Locate original sign from bond campaign.	
S. 2	Balloons for sign	D.	3/25/06	B. arranged for donation. D. pick up balloons.	Donated
S. 3	Put sign at corner	A.	3/25/06 Complete	EE. walked it down!	
T.	**Clean-up & Follow-up**	A.			
T. 1	Who	A.		A., B., D., KB, DD., whoever else is still standing!	
T. 2	Stage	KB		Y. to help	
T. 3	Tables	A.		Fold 'em up and pile off to the side	
T. 4	Trash	B.		Pull it all together and get dishes to kitchen area	
T. 5	Thank You	A. & CC.	By April 15, 2006	Cards & Stamps Purchased	6.00
T. 6	Retrieve "Join Us" sign	A.	By 3/28/06	The party's over . . . it was a hit then . . . :}	

Budget

	Task	$$s
A.	Secure Facilities	0.00
B.	Invitations	247.00
C.	Publicity	0.00
D.	Library Ready?	40.00
E.	Working that day?	0.00
F.	Food	52.00
G.	Tables	38.00
H.	Capture the Day	0.00
I.	Entertainment	100.00
J.	History of Library	0.00
K.	Copies Made	18.00
L.	Guest Book & Flip Charts	8.00
M.	Donation "Dog House"	8.00
N.	Chinese Auction	0.00
O.	Children's Time 2-4	15.00
P.	Vendors	0.00
Q.	Scottie Promotional Items	35.00
R.	Scottie Mascot Outfit	0.00
S.	Street Sign	0.00
T.	Clean-up & Follow-up	6.00
Total Anticipated Expenses		**567.00**

After the invitations the stage is the most expensive item. However, it will be used for future programs. It will be stored across the street and assembly directions will be on it, so future people can use it easily.

The cost of the invitations is the cost to make money. Why do this if no one knows?

The hours involved have not been calculated. It is anticipated that the staff may put in extra time above the normal work week. This decision will be left up to them. The general operating budget can handle the additional expense of this time. Also, volunteers will be asked to help when possible.

Evaluation

Beyond the goals and objectives listed previously. This project will be considered a success if the following occurs:

1. At least 200 people beyond the "normal library community" receive personal invitations.
2. Extra donations are received the day of the party. (Outside of the normal range of donations on a Saturday.)
3. Celtic collection begins to circulate.
4. A "good time" is reported by many post celebration.

These are successful for the following reasons:

Goal	Result/Outcome
✓ The celebration occurs on March 25, 2006. One time, with in budget and we have fun!	⇨ We did it! Stronger staff team for it. Board actually can and does get involved.
✓ At least 200 people out side of the "normal library community" receive personal invitations.	⇨ New Patrons. See an increase the next few weeks in new applications.
✓ Extra donations are received the day of the party. (Outside of the normal range of donations on a Saturday of $10.)	⇨ Above $100 will be a HUGE success. Granted, this will not cover the expenses of the party. But it will let us (board and staff) know that we can do this.
✓ Celtic collection begins to circulate.	⇨ Increased awareness of unique items for the community.
✓ A "good time" is reported by many who attended post celebration.	⇨ Word of mouth around town that good things are happening at the Scott Township Public Library. Can't pay for this type of publicity!

Flyers are a great way to provide information about your library to your patrons and the greater community. Scott Township Library has done a great job of creating flyers to keep users informed about services the library has to offer.

The library's "Welcome Flyer" provides information about hours and lending policies. Here's an example of their flyer. You may want to think about what you can do to market your library to patrons.

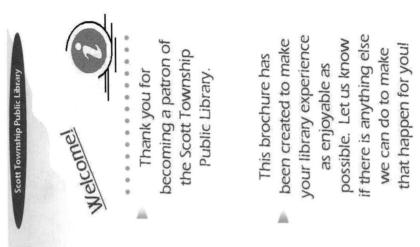

Scott Township Public Library

Welcome!

Thank you for becoming a patron of the Scott Township Public Library.

This brochure has been created to make your library experience as enjoyable as possible. Let us know if there is anything else we can do to make that happen for you!

Sincerely,
The Library Staff &
Janet Forton,
Director

A Scott Township Library card is your key to a universe of information and entertainment.

Cherish it, guard it, and use it wisely.

Patron Agreement: A library card permits the borrowing of valuable and expensive material that is public property which must be returned. The library card holder is financially responsible for library property charged out to his/her card. The parent/legal guardian who endorses a child's application is financially responsible for materials charged out to the minor (under the age of 18) child.

Law and the administrative policies of the Scott Township Public Library protect the confidentiality of library records. Library policies concerning confidentiality safeguard your rights to free speech and privacy. In order to safeguard access to library records, only the patron who owns the library card, or in the case of overdue or lost books, the parent / legal guardian of a minor will have access to his/her record upon verification of the library card number. All other information will be restricted to that which does not reveal the content.

A map of the library is available at the Circulation Desk.

Scott Township Public Library

301 Lindsay Rd.
Scott Twp., PA 15106

Phone: 412-429-5380
Fax: 412-429-5370

Website:

http://www.einetwork.net/scotttwp/

When, How Many, and Financial Responsibilities

Helpful Hint: Mark your calendar for when items need to be returned! Or attach the list we give you when you check items out.

HOURS

MONDAY	9:30 AM-8:00 PM
TUESDAY	9:30 AM-8:00 PM
WEDNESDAY	9:30 AM-8:00 PM
THURSDAY	9:30 AM-8:00 PM
FRIDAY	CLOSED
SATURDAY	9:30 AM-4:30 PM
SUNDAY	CLOSED

LENDING POLICIES

There is no limit on the number of items you may borrow at one time from our library. The only "limit to borrowing" is how many items you want to be responsible for!

(Note: Other libraries may have different limits.)

New Books:	1 Week
DVDs:	1 Week
Videos (VHS):	1 Week
Puzzles:	1 Week
CDs:	1 Week
Magazines:	1 Week
Books:	3 Weeks
Audio Books:	3 Weeks

OVERDUE FINES

(What you are financially responsible for if an item is returned late . . .)

DVDs/Videos:	$1.00/day
All other items:	.10¢/day

(Note: Other libraries may have different rates.)

P:\forms\library card applications\welcome.pub

You may also want to provide your patrons with information about how they can volunteer at your library. Here's an example of how Scott Township library does that:

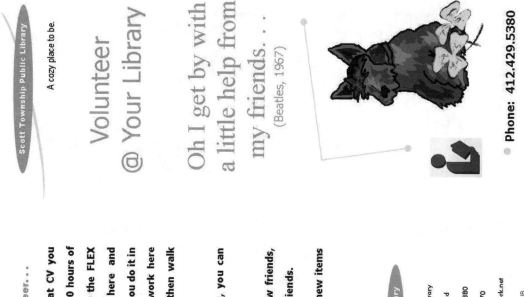

Scott Township Public Library

A cozy place to be.

Volunteer @ Your Library

Oh I get by with a little help from my friends. . . .
(Beatles, 1967)

Phone: 412.429.5380

More Reasons to Volunteer. . .

- If you are a student at CV you need to have at least 30 hours of community service for the FLEX Program. Volunteer here and get your hours in. (If you do it in the summer you can work here for an hour or 2 and then walk up to the pool!)

- If you are job hunting, you can add it to your resume.

- Network and make new friends, or reconnect with old friends.

- You get first crack at new items in the circulation.

Scott Township Public Library

Scott Township Library
301 Lindsay Road
Phone: 412-429-5380
Fax: 412-429-5370
Email: scott@einetwork.net

FORMS/VOLUNTEER @ YOUR LIBRARYPUB

Volunteers Make It Happen!

The Scott Township Public Library exists because of volunteers! For over 40 years dedicated volunteers pursued getting the township its own library. They finally saw that dream come true when the library opened its doors to the public on March 26, 2001, with just over 4,000 books on its shelves. The library has now grown to over 30,000 items that include books, newspapers, magazines, videos, and DVDs.

There are also a variety of programs offered for children and adults.

Volunteers for the library continue to be a key force in making us such a success! In 2005 we benefited from over 5,500 hours of volunteer time!

Do you have some time to share?

Sometimes libraries allow patrons to give a gift or donation in honor of a family member or friend. It's a great fundraising opportunity and it's meaningful to many people. Here's an informational flyer about this service from Scott Township Library:

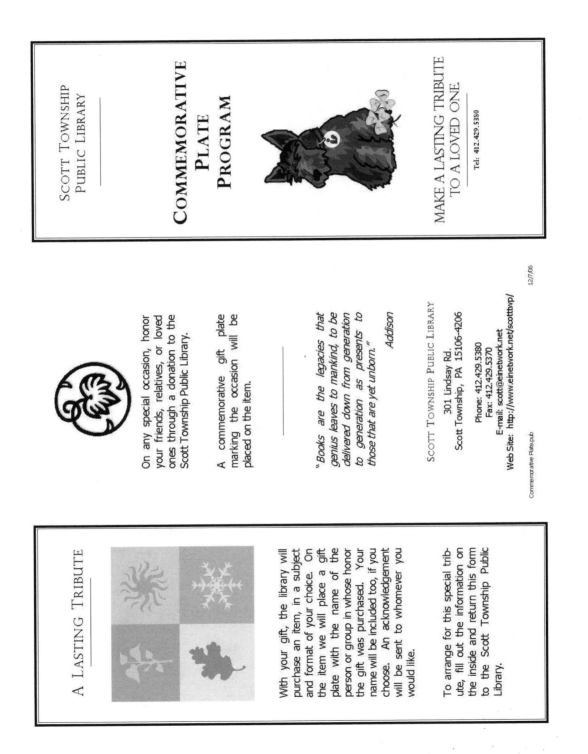

SCOTT TOWNSHIP
PUBLIC LIBRARY

COMMEMORATIVE
PLATE
PROGRAM

MAKE A LASTING TRIBUTE
TO A LOVED ONE.

Tel: 412.429.5380

On any special occasion, honor your friends, relatives, or loved ones through a donation to the Scott Township Public Library.

A commemorative gift plate marking the occasion will be placed on the item.

"Books are the legacies that genius leaves to mankind, to be delivered down from generation to generation as presents to those that are yet unborn."

Addison

SCOTT TOWNSHIP PUBLIC LIBRARY
301 Lindsay Rd.
Scott Township, PA 15106-4206

Phone: 412.429.5380
Fax: 412.429.5370
E-mail: scott@einetwork.net
Web Site: http://www.einetwork.net/scotttvp/

Commemorative Plate.pub

12/1/06

A LASTING TRIBUTE

With your gift, the library will purchase an item, in a subject and format of your choice. On the item we will place a gift plate with the name of the person or group in whose honor the gift was purchased. Your name will be included too, if you choose. An acknowledgement will be sent to whomever you would like.

To arrange for this special tribute, fill out the information on the inside and return this form to the Scott Township Public Library.

Libraries often conduct user surveys to get information about the community population and its needs. Scott Township Public Library recently created two surveys: one for patrons and one for teachers:

All information contained in this appendix is the property of Scott Township Library. For information, contact:

Janet B. Forton
Director, Scott Township Public Library
301 Lindsay Rd., Scott Township, PA 15106
(P) 412-429-5380
(F) 412-429-5370

Abington Library

Examples of the *Ideal Patron* posters are found in Appendix E. The Abington Library also has a newsletter that is a great marketing tool to highlight their events. See Appendix G.

Abington Community Library recently won a state marketing award from the Office of Commonwealth Libraries' Bureau of Library Development for excellence in promoting lifelong learning through its services and programs. One of the library's landmark marketing projects was its *Ideal Patron* campaign, an initiative designed for patron recognition during National Library Week.

Library users are given the opportunity to complete a survey about knowledge of library activities and to nominate a patron as an "ideal patron." This marketing campaign also included the creation of *Ideal Patron* posters, which feature real library patrons and promote awareness of library services and programs.

The *Ideal Patron* campaign is the intellectual property of the Abington Community Library. The photographs are the property of Guy Cali Photography, Clarks Summit, PA. For more information, contact:

Leah Ducato Rudolph, MLIS
Director Abington Community Library
Or
Gisela Butera, MLIS Candidate
1200 West Grove St.
Clarks Summit, PA 18411-9501
(570) 587-3440
lrudolph@albright.org

Appendix E

Poster Examples

THE IDEAL PATRON

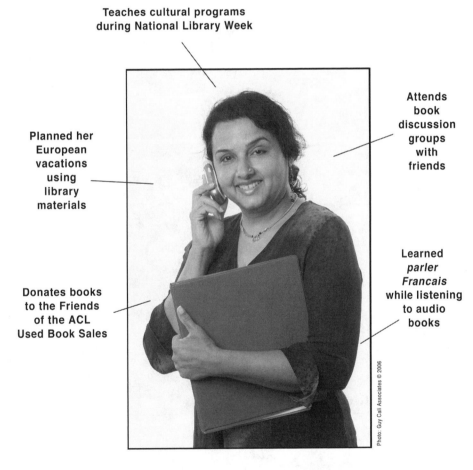

Teaches cultural programs
during National Library Week

Attends
book
discussion
groups
with
friends

Planned her
European
vacations
using
library
materials

Learned
*parler
Francais*
while listening
to audio
books

Donates books
to the Friends
of the ACL
Used Book Sales

Photo: Guy Cali Associates © 2006

1200 W. Grove St.
Clarks Summit, PA 18411
(570) 587-3440
www.lclshome.org/Abington

Committed to lifelong learning.

Abington
Community
Library
A Member of The
Lackawanna County
Library System

THE IDEAL PATRON

Uses the Interlibrary Loan
system for scholarly
research

Attended a book
discussion of
**The Westing
Game** for middle
school students

Uses online
services to
place holds
and renew
materials

Created an
abstract painting
during a fun
summer art
program

Attends family
programs at
the library

Photo: Guy Cali Associates © 2006

1200 W. Grove St.
Clarks Summit, PA 18411
(570) 587-3440
www.lclshome.org/Abington

Committed to lifelong learning.

Abington
Community
Library
A Member of The
Lackawanna County
Library System

THE IDEAL PATRON

Helps his grandson learn computer skills using educational games

His grandfather brings him to the library's annual 'Dirt Digger Day'

Researched theme parks online to find the best roller coasters to ride with his grandson

Enjoys the summer reading program

Volunteers to help at the Friends of the ALC Used Book Sales

Photo: Guy Cali Associates © 2006

1200 W. Grove St.
Clarks Summit, PA 18411
(570) 587-3440
www.lclshome.org/Abington

Committed to lifelong learning

Abington
Community
Library
A Member of The
Lackawanna County
Library System

Appendix F

Sample Annual Reports

Message from the Director

Year 2005 started on what most might think of as an unusual "note" for a library. Since the main library location had passed its 25th year of serving the public, it was time to update the restrooms with new equipment and a new look. The facelift went well and the public has much nicer facilities to use. By late fall the library would finally have a storage building to house equipment and tools. The architect for the Indian Creek Branch designed an attractive and useful building that includes sorting and storage space for OPL's Friends' organization as well. Many of you are familiar with the Friends' book sales and may even help out at the sales. Organizing for book sales requires storage and workspace. Now the Friends have plenty of space and ease in which to carry out their tasks!

Early 2005 also brought the launch of a completely new website for the library at www.olathelibrary.org. With the combined help of staff and a web designer, the library now has a more attractive and serviceable site. A helpful website greatly assists customers from work or home in a variety of ways with a calendar of programs, the library catalog, numerous databases and other helpful information.

During the summer the library hosted its annual Summer Reading Club offered to all ages. On kickoff day, May 31, the number of children signing up for SRC folders increased 15%! The library's theme, "Dragons, Dreams and Daring Deeds", attracted children to special programs and events. More emphasis was placed on reading, when library staff participated in the first "Kansas Reads to Preschoolers" by reading to preschoolers in and outside of the library during a special week in November. December carried through with reading emphasis when the library, the city and the school district officially began a cooperative effort, known as OLATHE READS, to promote literacy throughout the community.

By the end of the year, 1,319,971 checkouts of books, tapes and CDs were borrowed by 86,679 cardholders. June earned the designation of highest checkout month for 2005 with 130,442 materials loaned. Interlibrary loan between libraries increased 26.3%. Statistics continue to show that both the main library and the branch experience increased usage every year. The Olathe Public Library strives to meet the educational, informational and recreational needs of the community!

Emily Baker
Library Director

Board of Directors

Mike Rinke, President
Wes McCoy, Vice-President
Cathie Bennie, Secretary
Dana Campbell, Treasurer

Jack Hansen
Tom Hutcheson
Ray Morrison
Emily Baker, *Director*
Peggy Ingle, *Ex-Officio, President, Friends of OPL*
Clifford Tatham, *Ex-Officio, Chair, OPL Foundation*
Michael Copeland, *Ex-Officio, Mayor of Olathe*

2005 Highlights

The library originally launched its website in 1998. While that website served it purpose it was in need of a makeover which was accomplished in early 2005.

In late March of 2005, the library launched its new website. The new website offered an easier navigation scheme with a more consistent look and feel throughout the site.

OLATHE PUBLIC LIBRARY
WIRELESS

FREE SPOT

In 2005, the Olathe Public Library became a free Wi-Fi spot, making free wireless access available in both Olathe Public Library locations. Anyone with a laptop, PDA or other portable device with a wireless network card was able to connect to the Internet free of charge.

The shelving was expanded and in March, the Indian Creek Branch's circulation desk was dismantled, enlarged and reinstalled. This project was funded by the Friends of the Olathe Public Library.

Children's Highlights

In 2005, the Children's Department conducted 530 story times with 6285 in attendance and held 102 programs with 4311 in attendance.

Some highlights for the year included Paul Mesner Puppets presenting Aesop's Fabulous Tales and returning a few weeks later for a puppet workshop.

Children's singer Dino O'Dell performed at both libraries.

The new Read to A Dog program was enjoyed by children who read aloud to trained registered therapy dogs to help improve literacy.

The newly introduced Family Game Night encouraged families to bring their own games or use the games provided during this event.

The Summer Reading Kick-Off in the park was a success with games, music, refreshments and the opportunity to sign up for the summer reading program. The theme this year was "Dragons, Dreams and Daring Deeds."

Throughout the summer there were a variety of different programs where children listened to stories, enjoyed a magic show, and created art projects such as a dragon, knight's gear and the children

In the fall, there was a sleepover at the Main library where children arrived at the library after it closed on a Friday. Activities included relays, singing, reader's theatre, stories and pizza.

Teen's Highlights

A Chain Maille program was held in the spring. Teens learned about the art of chain maille and were given the opportunity to begin a project.

Workshops such as acting, jewelry making, juggling and magic were conducted throughout the year.

A teen lock-in was held in the fall as teens gathered at the library to eat pizza, play games and create art projects.

A duct tape workshop was conducted in the summer with a duct tape contest held at the end of the summer. There were many creative entries with the guitar receiving first prize.

A poetry, short story and bookmark contest was held. At the end of the contest, a party was held at the Café for the Birds where entrants gathered for pizza and pop. The winners were announced at the party and given an opportunity to read their work.

After the awards ceremony, young adult author Terry Trueman sat down with the teens for a question and answer session.

Circulation

Circulation

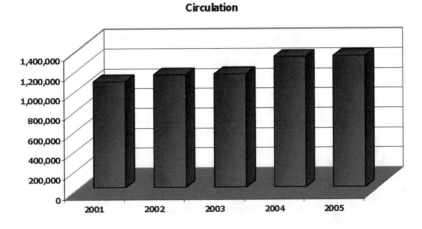

In 2004, the Olathe Public Library circulated 1,305,594 items. In 2005, the library circulated 1,319,971 an increase of 14,377 items over the previous year.

Library Visits

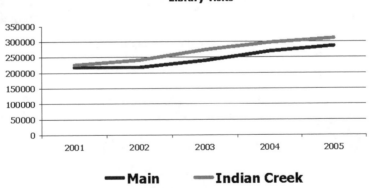

In 2005, there was a combined 598,070 library visits, marking a 6% increase over 2004. In the past five years, the libraries combined have realized a 35% increase in the number of library visits.

Friends of Olathe Public Library

The Friends of the Olathe Public Library continue to be a solid support group for the library. During 2005, the group provided funds to support the children's summer reading program – providing a free paperback book to each of the 825 children that completed the program. It boosted the library's collection by giving $2,000 to enhance the documentary DVD and $1,000 for the music CD collections. An additional $2,770 was given to the library for furniture to house the growing music CD collection and the group once again gave $2,000 to the OPL Foundation. A $500 grant was given to the Young Adult Program and the Friends purchased new magazine binders for the main library. The Friends continued to pay for a subscription to the "Chapter a Day" online book club

Friends hosted five "mini" book sales at the Indian Creek Branch meeting room with proceeds totaling $5000 and also organized two Ella Mae Memorial Book Sales in April and October, generating around $10,000 in sales and membership dues. The sale of Friends book bags in-house generated over $400 for the year.

The Friends-sponsored dinner in April drew a large crowd to enjoy a presentation, "Romance of the Road: Traveling Across Kansas," by Sue Suellentrop from the Kansas Humanities Council.

During 2005, 108 baby board books were given to Olathe parents of newborns. The Friends provide the books for this project.

A new Friends group, PALS (Parents Promoting Awareness of Library Services), was formed to support the activities and mission of Children's Services in the library. The Friends group awarded PALS a $250 grant to get started.

Friends Board

Peggy Ingle, President
Tom Hutcheson, Secretary
Carlotta Belcher, Membership

Shirley Grove, Vice-President
Jeanne Becker, Treasurer
Cindy Miller, Newsletter

Volunteers

	Number of Volunteers	Number of Hours
2001	341	6316
2002	438	6625
2003	609	8540
2004	538	9358
2005	426	7589

In April, eighty volunteers, guests and library staff members gathered at the Deaf Cultural Center for the annual Volunteer Recognition Reception.   Attendees enjoyed a light supper, followed by a prize drawing and awarding of certificates to the youth volunteers.

This year, three outstanding volunteers were recipients of the Nancy Quinlisk Chandler Award. Clarence (A.D.) Admire, a volunteer since 1985, presently sorts and prices the book sale materials. Mike Foubert works with Admire and has been a volunteer for eleven years. The final recipient was Ray Morrison, who has been a member of the Olathe Public Library Board of Directors since 1995, serving as secretary and president.

Olathe Public Library Foundation

In 2005, people flocked to the third annual Lobster Fest. Whitney Terrell, author of *The King of Kings County* and *The Huntsman* was the speaker.

During the evening, grants were awarded to the children's department —$2,000 for easy DVDs and books on CD as well as $1,000 for children's furniture & $1,000 for Young Adult Programming.

In addition, the foundation gave grants of $2160 for movie performance rights, $250 for juvenile books and $500 for KLTA continuing education for trustees.

The foundation hosted its first ice cream social in conjunction with the Friends Book Sale. The endeavor raised $284.

Foundation Board

Cliff Tatham (Chair)   Emily Baker
Dana Campbell   Diane Costello
Micki Holliday   Peggy Ingle
Sandy Waters   Pam Wilkinson

Financial Summary

Personnel	$2,186,330
Books & Materials	489,059
Utilities	56,517
Supplies	73,818
Building	108,827
Automation	187,955
Copiers	8,264
Insurance	32,589
Equipment	24,929
Staff Development	17,025
Library Vehicle	2,184
Printing	3,079
Professional Services	18,132
Miscellaneous	23,104
Programming	12,898
Capital Improvement	215,134
Total Expenses	**$3,459,844**

Income Received

Tax Revenue	$3,319,281
Interest Income	46,080
Fines, Copier, Misc.	134,698
Contributions	29,159
Total	**$3,529,218**

State Aid Received and Expended

State Aid	$73,372
Interlibrary Loan	
Development Grant	8,226
Total	**$81,598**

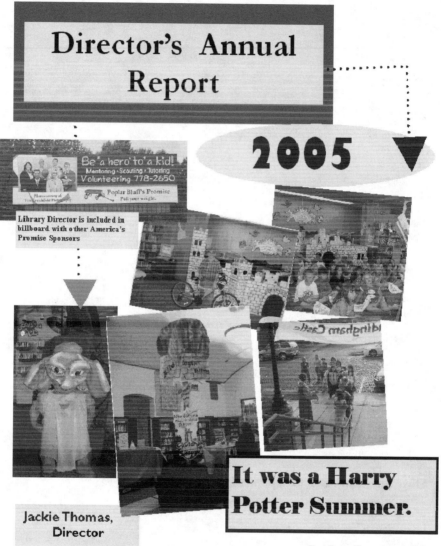

Director's Annual Report

2005

Be 'a hero' to' a kid!
Mentoring · Scouting · Tutoring
Volunteering 778-2650

Poplar Bluff's Promise
Pull your weight.

Library Director is included in
billboard with other America's
Promise Sponsors

Jackie Thomas,
Director

It was a Harry
Potter Summer.

Next Page · More about the Library

Poplar Bluff Public Library
2005 Director's Annual Report

The following goals were set for

- Add a part time technology support person. *—this past year has proven to everyone, that technology is not a one person job.*
- Establish an equipment line item in the budget—*this was lost this year when State Aid was included with other 401 general fund revenues.*
- Paint needed on interior walls in the library—*some ceilings are badly stained from water damaged over several years. The new wing receives a high amount of traffic and is beginning to show wear on the walls and ceilings.*
- Address maintenance issues, listed previously, as quickly as money is available—*this list is long. And the old saying "the wheel that squeaks the loudest gets the most oil" applies to repairs.*
- Send/encourage staff to attend seminars and conferences—*this boosts morale and energizes the entire staff. It often saves money and time, when staff return with ideas.*
- Attend the National ALA/PLA meeting—*I have missed these meetings a great deal. They allow me to view the library from a different perspective. Sometimes I feel I can't see the forest, because of all the trees.*
- Install a bifold door or similar type door in the large community room separating the room in half.—*This will allow double booking of the room and more efficient use of space.*
- Resolve staffing hours issue in the children's department—*the number of hours needed in the children's department has increased. An evaluation of the staff and projects is needed.*
- Keep personnel cost at 70% of the budget—*this is difficult, but with an increase in salaries and none in operating, it is probably impossible.*
- To write a long term plan (3-5 years) for the Library with the assistance of the Library Board of Trustees—*to have a vision motivates and keeps everyone on track. Otherwise we just put out fires every year.*
- To set priorities early in the budget year—*the Board's input in setting budget priorities is essential. Trying to regulate the building maintenance budget has been very difficult.*

Poplar Bluff Public Library
2005 Director's Annual Report

Summary

The 2005 year may have been 365 days in length, but those days must have been the shortest days in history. A year has never gone so quickly.

The spirit and speed for 2005 began with an early morning phone call on October 27, 2004 from John Stanard. I was driving to St. Louis to attend the state library conference and answered on my cell phone. John told me about the Kay Porter gift for almost a million dollars— $980,000 to be exact. The next event I remember was greeting 125 children for the Harry Potter night celebration on June 15th. That was followed by the Board of Trustees Retreat on October 8, 2005. Where did all the time go? It was just a blur between those events. This year was so different from 2004 when staff morale was poor. No raises were given. Insurance was slashed and staff was lost. BUT, the year 2005 was a turn-around year and a major "high" for all the staff. Morale was up again. The Kay Porter Gift started the year with high spirits and lots of promise of things to come. Gee, what a year.

Goals for 2006 were not included in this annual report. After looking at the programming already planned for next year, it is my belief that no other goals can be realistically set. The library's 90th year celebration will consume everyone's time and energy. Of course, staff have already generated more ideas and goals than we can possibly achieve.

Several budget issues were resolved in 2005. A staff salary schedule was submitted and approved. The equipment line item was reinstated. The successful reinstatement of these two budget items is directly related to the positive involvement and commitment of the Library Board of Trustees.

The Library Board of Trustees, in my estimation, made a greater impact on the daily operation, staff morale, and library infrastructure during 2005 than any other year I have served as director. Thanks to all the members of the Board and a special thank you to those who served as officers during 2005.

I thought 2005 would be a difficult year to surpass, but 2006 is already off to a great start. Happy 90th Anniversary to the Poplar Bluff Public Library. Let's celebrate!

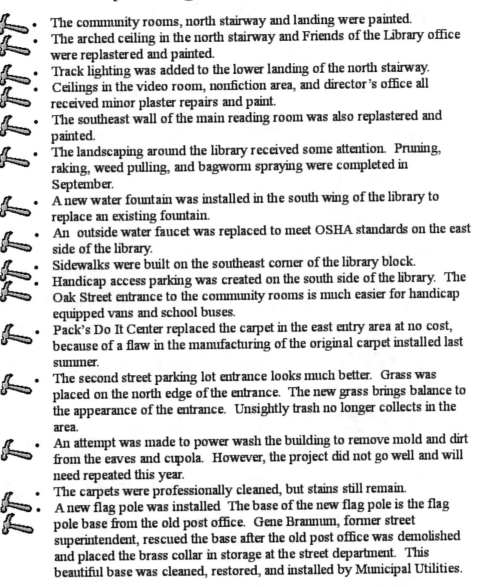

Poplar Bluff Public Library
2005 Director's Annual Report

Library Building Maintenance—the Highlights!!!

- The community rooms, north stairway and landing were painted.
- The arched ceiling in the north stairway and Friends of the Library office were replastered and painted.
- Track lighting was added to the lower landing of the north stairway.
- Ceilings in the video room, nonfiction area, and director's office all received minor plaster repairs and paint.
- The southeast wall of the main reading room was also replastered and painted.
- The landscaping around the library received some attention. Pruning, raking, weed pulling, and bagworm spraying were completed in September.
- A new water fountain was installed in the south wing of the library to replace an existing fountain.
- An outside water faucet was replaced to meet OSHA standards on the east side of the library.
- Sidewalks were built on the southeast corner of the library block.
- Handicap access parking was created on the south side of the library. The Oak Street entrance to the community rooms is much easier for handicap equipped vans and school buses.
- Pack's Do It Center replaced the carpet in the east entry area at no cost, because of a flaw in the manufacturing of the original carpet installed last summer.
- The second street parking lot entrance looks much better. Grass was placed on the north edge of the entrance. The new grass brings balance to the appearance of the entrance. Unsightly trash no longer collects in the area.
- An attempt was made to power wash the building to remove mold and dirt from the eaves and cupola. However, the project did not go well and will need repeated this year.
- The carpets were professionally cleaned, but stains still remain.
- A new flag pole was installed The base of the new flag pole is the flag pole base from the old post office. Gene Brannum, former street superintendent, rescued the base after the old post office was demolished and placed the brass collar in storage at the street department. This beautiful base was cleaned, restored, and installed by Municipal Utilities.

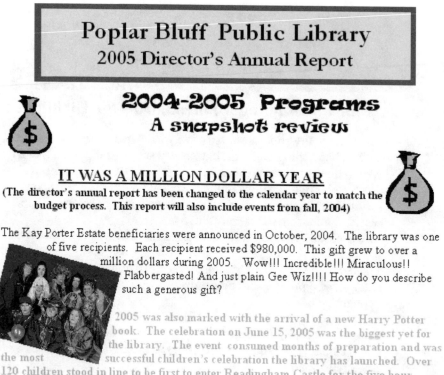

Poplar Bluff Public Library
2005 Director's Annual Report

2004-2005 Programs
A snapshot review

IT WAS A MILLION DOLLAR YEAR
(The director's annual report has been changed to the calendar year to match the budget process. This report will also include events from fall, 2004)

The Kay Porter Estate beneficiaries were announced in October, 2004. The library was one of five recipients. Each recipient received $980,000. This gift grew to over a million dollars during 2005. Wow!!! Incredible!!! Miraculous!! Flabbergasted! And just plain Gee Wiz!!!! How do you describe such a generous gift?

2005 was also marked with the arrival of a new Harry Potter book. The celebration on June 15, 2005 was the biggest yet for the library. The event consumed months of preparation and was the most successful children's celebration the library has launched. Over 120 children stood in line to be first to enter Readingham Castle for the five hour event.

Dragons, Dreams and Daring Deeds
was the perfect theme for the 2005 summer reading program. Many of the materials from the Harry Potter celebration were used again during the Summer Reading Program, The end of the summer program brought a great deal of laughter. A special laugh was heard when staff climbed the ladder and were DUNKED into some really gross looking water!!

STAFF attended out of town workshops and
seminars. Kay attended an all day interlibrary loan workshop in Cape Girardeau. Fredia attended two different children's workshops in the area and Ron Harrison attended a week long library conference in Columbia, Missouri. Jackie attended Missouri Public Library Director meetings in June and December and was appointed to the executive committee of the MPLD association as treasurer. All staff participated in online training courses through the University of North

Poplar Bluff Public Library
2005 Director's Annual Report

Earth Day was celebrated in April. The children's librarian worked closely with the Parks and Recreation Department to entertain the children all month long with stories about our earth and how to care for it. Children were also given a free planting from the George O White Nursery. The month was so successful, that the theme will be repeated this April.

Participation in the Fourth of July parade was a first for the staff and they brought home a trophy. 2nd prize was awarded to the library and the money was deposited into the gift account. Other float participants claimed that if the library didn't win an award from the judges, then they would award us an award for the most "fun" group to be in the parade. Dennis Keeney loaned his beautiful bass boat and truck. Dennis is convinced that the boat won the prize. The theme for the float was "get hooked on books."

The 3rd annual Read and Ride Program sponsored by 1st Midwest Bank provided three very luck children new bikes this summer. Tucker Davis, liaison with the bank, is always eager to say yes to this program.

Rotary Club of Poplar Bluff awarded the library a grant of $5,000 which added "**SIX**" new public computers to the library. Equipment grants from the federal and state governments have disappeared within the past two years. Money is now being targeted away from equipment and toward literacy programs.

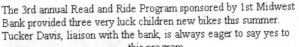

The Library celebrates Dr. Seuss' birthday each year with a party for the children. This year was extra special, because young adults from the Sears Youth Center joined in the fun and helped the children really enjoy themselves.

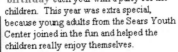

2005 Annual Report

Poplar Bluff Public Library
2005 Director's Annual Report

Masters of the Sky from the World Bird Sanctuary in St. Louis visited the children during the summer program. The Parks and Recreation Department and Friends of the Library cosponsored one of the most popular events of the summer. Two performances were attended by over 200 children and adults.

Children were also entertained by magician and his magic dragons. The magician is an annual program provided each year by the Friends of the Library as part of the summer reading program.

Boys and Girls Club program finally "took off" this year. After attempting several approaches, this year's program is really working. A big thank you to the children's librarian. She visits

every Tuesday afternoon . She works individually with each child to select books which are grade appropriate. She has also been guilty of taking over some comic books!!!   children's cards

Over 40 new have been issued since the program began in September.

Harry Potter took a great deal of time and lots of children enjoyed the celebration. Mrs. Porter

Poplar Bluff Public Library
2005 Director's Annual Report

Children's Fall Reading Program ended with a
ZOORIFIC BASH.
A puppet show, reading den, zoo cafeteria, elephant games, balls tossed through hoops, and prizes kept children and parents entertained for almost two hours on Friday evening October 28, 2005.

Children's programming continued to the very end of the year.

- A HARRY POTTER drawing was held in November. Children won calendars and posters to celebrate the release of the newest Harry Potter movie.

- The children's library celebrated the CHRONICLES OF NARNIA; THE LION, THE WITCH, AND THE WARDROBE movie release with a party on December 16th. Two lucky children received complete sets of the CHRONICLES OF NARNIA books by C.S. Lewis.

- To wrap up the year—toddlers and preschoolers participated in the MISSOURI PICTURE BLOCK AWARD PROGRAM sponsored each year by the Missouri Library Association. The program selects ten children's picture books for preschoolers each year. The children vote after reading the books for their favorite title from the list. Authors who win this award are especially blessed, because the children have selected the winner.

2005 Annual Report

John Stanard's author signing event held on December 15, 2005 was a great success with over $500 in sales for the single day. John's BUTLER COUNTY: A PICTORIAL HISTORY Vols. 1 & 2 have been available at the library since 1999. This year's sales grossed more than $1,000.

Next Page - **Previous Page** - **More about the Library**

Poplar Bluff Public Library
2005 Director's Annual Report

ISSUES AND CONCERNS

Points which are proceeded by a "bullet" have appeared on previous annual reports

- Two **exterior lights** on the north wing, which are original to the building, need attention. The north wing is on the National Historic Register and will impact how these lights are restored or replaced.

- **New carpeting** is needed in several areas of the library. Stains and heavy traffic are beginning to show dirt and deep wear patterns.

- The existing **fire and smoke alarm system** is not practical and needs replaced.

- **Video security** should be installed in the library.

- One of the most difficult maintenance issues is the replacement of the light bulbs and ballasts in the LARGE GLOBE ceiling lights in the library.

The age of the building is beginning to require **more hours of preventive maintenance and routine cleaning**. The budget for the cleaning and maintenance of the building has not been increased in several years.

The Main Street step railings are in need of repair. Although, there appears to be no safety problem, the rust on the railings is becoming quite noticeable.

The staff entrance door needs to be readjusted or realigned. The locking mechanisms no longer are in alignment which results in the door not being properly locked.

Poplar Bluff Public Library
2005 Director's Annual Report

JUST THE FACTS

What did it take to run the Poplar Bluff Public Library in 2005?
The following are some interesting FACTS!

- It took approximately 303 days or 2,800 hours to keep the doors open Monday through Saturday
- It took approximately 11,400 man hours
- Staff handled each book approximately 5 times for each completed transaction. This resulted in the staff pushing, shoving, lifting and carrying almost 800,000 items
- Over 108,412 people visited the library during the past year.
- Staff provided over 100 combined years of library experience
- Staff walked approximately 4,300 miles to provide service
- Staff answered approximately 24,284 reference questions
- Children' staff checked out almost 50,000 items
- 626 people attended adult programs
- Over 1,954 children attended programs
- 13,370 active borrowers used library cards
- The library spent almost $2,000 replacing light bulbs in all the ceiling lights
- $40,500 was spent on print and nonprint books and information
- The front doors to the library were locked and unlocked 606 times
- Staff turned computers on and off at least 17,574 times.
- Children printed out 1,900 pages of homework at no charge
- 7,780 large print books were checked out
- Patrons used the online book clubs over 10,260 times
- Adult computers surfed the internet over 18,264 times
- It took over 3,000 running feet of book shelves to hold all the books circulated
- Patrons used the online library book collection over 1,085 times
- Patrons kept the microfilm machines on for more than 6,000 hours
- The phone was answered more than 30,000 times

Reading Public Library
Annual Report 2005

The Reading Public Library is at the heart of an involved, articulate, and literate community.

The library:
- Anticipates the ever changing needs of the community
- Seeks innovative ways to provide and enhance library services
- Leads the way in building a diverse and vibrant community.

The Reading Public Library serves the community from birth through old age.   Through its collections, programs, and outreach activities, it supports and encourages reading and learning, intellectual curiosity, personal growth and development.

In 2005, Reading citizens borrowed 372,456 print and audiovisual materials from the Library - almost 16 books for every man, woman, and child in Reading! The Reading Public Library is the busiest library per hour in its population group in the Northeast Region. 17,381 Reading residents, 74% of the town, have current library cards!

The library collects, preserves, and promotes the study of local history. The library borrows and shares resources with libraries throughout Massachusetts. In 2005, 22,639 books were borrowed for local residents.

The Children's Room presented 321 programs to 14,184 children in 2005. Chess, filmmaking, poetry writing, Harry Potter midnight party, live theatre productions, live animals, Vehicle Day, and more, were educational as well as fun!

200 storytimes and singalongs this year fostered the love of language and stories in children from 0-6 years of age. Especially in Lapsits for ages 0-2, librarians help caregivers learn the basics of early literacy and what they can do to best help their children develop good reading skills in the future.

To encourage personal growth and community involvement, our Summer Volunteen program for middle schoolers helped 75 students help others by their work in the Library.

The Reading Public Library teaches adults and children how to find, evaluate, and use information effectively in all formats.

Reference Librarians instruct individuals and groups

A series of free evening classes kicked off in 2005. Adults enjoyed "Mousing Around," using the Internet for making travel plans, shopping, and accessing reliable sources for Health Information. "Geek Out, Don't Freak Out!" provided patrons an opportunity to bring their newest gadgets to the library and work with staff to figure out how to use them. Digital cameras were definitely the most popular and most challenging new toy!

Geek Out - Don't Freak Out! at the Library

The library provides a learning environment for the digital world and the equipment, connections, and resources to ensure an excellent learning experience. Many patrons took advantage of the library's Wireless connectivity to log in to the Internet using their own laptops in the library.

Librarians provide instruction in library resources in formal classes, through individual one on one teaching, and with local school groups. Every eighth-grader in the Parker and Coolidge Schools participated in the annual "Cookie Tours" given by the Young Adult

librarians with funding provided by the Friends of the Library and with the cooperation, support, and active encouragement of school faculty and administration.

1234 Children joined the Summer Reading Club & Read for 18,520 Hours

The Reading Public Library provides collections that respond to community needs to help fulfill community residents' needs for education, entertainment, and enlightenment.

The circulation of video and audio materials locally has soared from 11% of total circulation in 1995 to 30% in 2005.

What are the hot topics in Reading this year? Books on home additions, cooking, finance, knitting, mysteries, and "Chick Lit!"

The Reading Public Library provides an environment for people to meet and interact with others in the community and to participate in public discourse about community issues. We strive to make everyone in the community feel welcome and well-served at the library.

"Word of Mouth" Group's monthly book review

15,878 adults and children took part in 446 library programs in 2005.

By providing resources and programs for people of all ages, the library contributes to the vitality of the community, supports education, and functions as a place for family enrichment.

Vehicle Day! An annual tradition

One of the highlights of the past year was the appearance of Pulitzer Prize-winning author Tracy Kidder in November, sponsored by the Reading Public Library Foundation, that drew several hundred people. Tom Perrotta (author of the bestseller, *Little Children*) also spoke at the Library's annual Open House in March. Mitali Perkins addressed a summer audience of young adults about her life and work as a person of Indian American heritage.

The Library reached out to new populations in 2005 through a federally funded grant to develop a book and audio visual collection for people who read Chinese, Hindi, and Spanish. The 522 books, tapes, newspapers and magazines and ESOL materials have circulated

1,793 times to date. Programs included World Music, Chinese puppets, Indian dance, a family fiesta and a world travel club with "trips" to Peru, Tanzania and India.

The library offers topical programs and information for everyday life, like programs on electronic shopping, health information, and the Active Older Adults Fair, in cooperation with many community partners and agencies.

Volunteers Help With Taxes

In 2005, staff librarians at the Reference and Children's desks answered an astonishing 52,158 questions in person, on the phone, and through email. Where else but at the Reading Public Library can you find a resource like that?

Thank you!

The library is generously supported by the people of Reading and the Selectmen, Town Manager, and the Library's Trustees, Foundation, and Friends. Books, programs, outreach services, and special performances are underwritten by the gifts and hard work of many kind supporters and benefactors. We thank you all for your essential contribution to the community. Without your generosity, our success in serving Reading would be impossible!

Waiting for midnight & the new Harry Potter!

Appendix G

Sample Newsletters

CHECK it Out

JANUARY 2007

A MONTHLY
PUBLICATION
OF THE
BOZEMAN
PUBLIC
LIBRARY

626 East Main
Bozeman, MT 59715
582-2400
TDD 582-2301

www.bozemanlibrary.org

HOURS:

Mon.	10am-8pm
Tue.	10am-8pm
Wed.	10am-8pm
Thurs.	10am-8pm
Fri.	10am-5pm
Sat.	10am-5pm
Sun.	1pm-5pm
	(Sept.-May)

Library Board
Ron Farmer, Chair
Al Kesselheim
Holly Brown
Marilyn King

Director
Alice Meister

*Friends of
Bozeman
Public Library*
John Gallagher,
President

*Library
Foundation*
522-9900
Chris Mehl,
President

*Library Publicity
and
Newsletter*
Cindy Christin

Farewell to Peg Hileman

Former Bozeman Public Library Director Peg Hileman was honored at our holiday party for volunteers in December. Peg was Director from 1950 - 1983, and continued to be an active volunteer several days a week until recently. Peg is moving to Alabama in January to be close to her family. Many of Peg's friends and fellow librarians attended the

event, sharing stories of early days at the Library, hiking trips, and other memories. The photo above shows Peg next to the Information Desk, which an anonymous donor named in her honor. We will miss Peg shelving books, reading *Calvin and Hobbes* and mysteries during lunch, and her stories of her cat. Best of luck, Peg!

String Trio Performs January 16

The Library is excited to announce that the Bozeman Symphony String Trio will perform on Tuesday, January 16 at 7 p.m. in the large

Community Room. We are the lucky recipient of a free Far Afield performance offered by the Bozeman Symphony in communities throughout Montana. Funding is provided through grants from Mountain Sky Guest Ranch, the Dennis & Phyllis Washington Foundation, the Montana Assoc. of Symphony Orchestras, and the Montana Cultural Trust.

The Bozeman Symphony String Trio is composed of the Symphony's principal string players. Carrie Krause on violin, Mary Carson on viola, and Chandra Lind on cello will perform a classical and energetic repertoire for an audience of all ages. Please join us for this special winter event at your new Library!

Martin Luther King Celebration

The Library will be involved in two events in honor of Martin Luther King Jr. this year. The celebration begins with a march down Main Street on Sunday, January 14 beginning at the Imperial Inn at noon and ending at the Library. The march is to commemorate Dr. King's work and the 1963 March on Washington D.C. If you would like to participate, meet in the Imperial Inn parking lot at 12:00. Following the march we will have educational stations and displays inside the Library dedicated to Dr. King's work, including video presentations, CD listening stations, music, and other events to be announced.

We will also have an evening program on Monday, January 15 at 7 p.m. to honor Martin Luther King, Jr. The celebration will include speakers, music and refreshments.

If you are interested in helping with the event, please call the Library at 582-2420, or you can contact Ruth Forrest at 579-7649.

Library Lighting

In last month's newsletter, we mentioned that we "are working with the contractor to increase the amount of light." This was never a contractor problem; it was a design and budget issue. Stack lights along the high shelves were eliminated from the budget due to the high cost, nearly $205,000. The lighting subcontractor assured us that even with the stack lights gone there would be adequate light levels in the library. We'll keep you informed as we work to resolve the lighting problem. In the meantime, we encourage your comments and suggestions regarding your new building. Please fill out a suggestion form at the Information Desk, or click on the link on our homepage at www.bozemanlibrary.org.

Book Club Meets Jan. 3

The Library Book Club meets on Wednesday, January 3, 2007 at 7:30 p.m. in the small Conference Room to discuss the newest Tom McGuane title, *Gallatin Canyon: Stories.* One reviewer says that this new collection of stories suggests that short fiction may be McGuane's true calling. Most of the stories depict desperate men well past their midlife crises set in Montana, Michigan and Florida. All interested readers are invited to this informal discussion. The Book Club is free and open to the public. Books to check out are available at the Reference Desk.

Great Decisions Meets

Please join us for the monthly Great Decisions Foreign Policy Discussion Group, which will meet on Thursday, January 18 at 7 p.m. in the Conference Room. This month's topic is the Middle East: the war in Iraq, Iran's nuclear program, the conflict in Lebanon, and Israeli-Palestinian negotiations. You can read about how these issues shape the Middle East in the 2007 Briefing Book. These books will be available for purchase, or to check out, at the Reference Desk upstairs in the Library. The group is open to all. Great Decisions is sponsored by the Friends of the Library and the Montana Center for International Visitors (MCIV).

Film Professor Speaks

The International Speaker Series will feature MSU Film Professor Walter Metz on Thursday, January 25 at 7 p.m. in the large Community Room. The title of the lecture is "Contemporary Iranian Cinema." In this lecture filled with video clips, Dr. Metz will use our understanding of post-World War II Italian neo-realism as a way of introducing contemporary Iranian cinema, one of the most artistically vibrant national cinemas of the early 21st century. This unique program, sponsored by the Friends of the Library and the Montana Center for International Visitors, is free and open to the public.

Kids' Book Group

The Kids' Book Group will meet on Wednesday, January 24 at 4:15 p.m. to talk about *Secret of the Three Treasures,* a new chapter book by Janni Lee Simner. Elementary school student Tiernay West is a wonderfully eccentric character who is determined to find buried treasure, become a true adventurer, and right past wrongs. One reviewer says, "Tiernay is an irrepressible role model in her unwavering self-confidence, intellectual curiosity, and sense of humor." Readers age 8 and up are invited to join the group, and parents are welcome too. We'll meet in the student corner of the Children's Room for an informal discussion and snacks. Please call 582-2404 for more information.

Winnie-the-Pooh Party

A.A. Milne, author of the classic Winnie-the-Pooh books, was born on January 18, 1882. To celebrate his birthday, the Library will host another Winnie-the-Pooh Party on Saturday, January 20 at 11 a.m. in the large Community Room. Kids can bring their favorite characters for games, crafts, and bread and honey.

Library Tours

If your group or organization would be interested in a tour of the new building, please call the Information Desk at 582-2427. The Library has several volunteers who are able to take people on a behind-the-scenes tour of the building, and talk about the architecture, building materials, green features, and other unique aspects of the new Library.

Classes and groups of students can schedule tours on Monday mornings or afternoons by calling the Children's Desk at 582-2404. Floor plans and information about the building are also available for all patrons at the Information Desk.

Library Legislative Day

Several of our Library staff will be traveling to Helena on Tuesday, January 9 for Library Legislative Day in the capital. In addition to visiting the Legislature during the day, librarians are invited to meet and socialize with representatives at a reception at the State Library that evening. It gives librarians throughout the state an opportunity to meet the decision-makers in Helena and to learn more about current legislative issues and ongoing programs to benefit libraries.

Thank You for Gifts

The Library appreciates the recent donations of gently-used books, periodicals and audio/video materials. Many of these items are added to the circulating collection. Others are put in the Friends of the Library book sale. Proceeds from the Friends of the Library sales benefit the Library in many ways. Stop by Wild Joe's Coffee Shop in the main lobby to see the wonderful display of books that are currently for sale.

To help the Library staff and Friends, please consider the following before bringing donated materials to the Library:

• Keep the boxes light (under 40 pounds)

• Only recent textbooks of popular subjects can be accepted

• Please bring only items that are in good physical condition

• Current issue magazines (2005-2006) will be placed in the free material bin in the lobby (no catalogs please)

If you have questions, please call the Library at 582-2402.

> The Library will be closed on Monday, January 15, 2006 in honor of Martin Luther King, Jr. Day.
> Please join us for a Celebration in the Community Room at 7 p.m.

Library Lights

Winter Issue, 2006

Roselle Public Library Newsletter

Serving Roselle since 1940

HOURS:
Monday through Thursday
9:30 a.m. to 9:00 p.m.
Friday and Saturday
9:30 a.m. to 5:00 p.m.
Sunday
1:00 p.m. to 5:00 p.m.
630-529-1641

www.roselle.lib.il.us
www.catalog.roselle.lib.il.us

LIBRARY CLOSED
Wednesday November 22nd
close early—5pm

Thursday, November 23rd
Thanksgiving Day

Sunday, December 24th
Christmas Eve

Monday, December 25th
Christmas Day

Sunday, December 31st
New Year's Eve

Monday, January 1st, 2007
New Year's Day

Donation from the Taste of Roselle Commission

The Taste of Roselle Commission voted at the October, 2006 meeting to donate $2,500 for new shelf ends and displayers for the Roselle Public Library. After another successful Taste of Roselle in August, 2006, the Commission donated a percentage of the revenue earned to Roselle public services. The Library Board is grateful to receive this generous donation.

Library Has a New Young Adult Librarian

Stop by the Reference Desk and say hi to the Library's newest addition, Lori Matesic, Reference/ Young Adult Librarian. Lori comes to us from Pittsburgh, Pennsylvania and is a recent graduate of the University of Pittsburgh School of Information Sciences. In addition to providing reference service, Lori will be working with the Library's Young Adult patrons. Watch for new services and facilities geared toward this very important user group.

Commemorative Gift Program

The Commemorative Gift Program of the Roselle Public Library is a meaningful way to honor or remember a person, a group, an occasion, or a milestone. The following items have been presented as Commemorative Gifts during the Fall, 2006 season:

⇒ 1-year subscription to *Dig* magazine and a 1-year subscription to *Archaeology Today* magazine. Donated by Amy Cawley.
⇒ *Sequence* by Lori Andrews. Donated by Deborah Dechinistso.
⇒ Twenty Dollars toward Library Coffee Fund. Donated by Ethel Rathe

Trustee News

Margorie Engel announced that she will resign her position as Library Trustee effective when the Board of Trustees fills her vacancy in November, 2006. Marge has served two separate terms as Library Trustee; one from 1969 to 1975 during which she served as Board Secretary and Board President and the other from May, 2005 to present. The Library Board is grateful for her years of service to the Library.

It is the mission of the Roselle Public Library District to provide people of the community with the widest possible access to both educational and recreational information while increasing awareness of the library and its services.

Adult Services

Unless otherwise noted, register for these programs by phone, in person or online beginning November 13th

DICKENS AND 'A CHRISTMAS CAROL'
SUNDAY, DECEMBER 3 AT 1:30 P.M.
Join Linda Putnam, a London expert, tour guide and member of the Dickens Society for a slide presentation on this beloved Christmas tale. Linda discusses what might have inspired Dickens to write this tale, the social situations in 1843 England that appear in the story, and much more.

SECRETS OF SELLING ON EBAY, MADE EASY
TUESDAY, JANUARY 23 AT 7:00 P.M.
Learn the basics of selling on eBay© with Vivienne Porter of C³ Solutions. The program covers establishing a sellers account, tips on photographing your items, item descriptions, and how to use Turbo Lister software. All this will be done live on-line and by the end of the lecture an actual item will be up for auction.

SHARING, SAVING AND SCRAPBOOKING WITH DIGITAL IMAGES
THURSDAY, JANUARY 25, 2007, 7:00 P.M.
Would you like to share your digital pictures with loved ones via the Internet? Would you like to edit, organize, and print your photos? This presentation will help you organize and learn to work with digital images including printing them as well as making calendars, holiday cards, and gifts for the special people in you life. Join professional photographer Roger Mattingly for this interactive session with real world solutions to help you get the most from your camera, computer and software.

OUTER SOLAR SYSTEM –
PLANETS AND MISSIONS
TUESDAY, JANUARY 30, 2007, 7:00 P.M.
Join Jim Kovac, Jet Propulsion Labs Solar System Ambassador, for an informative presentation on the outer solar system. Mr. Kovac will discuss the journey outward from the Sun, to the realm of the gas giants. Jupiter, Saturn, Uranus, and Neptune not only offer surprises and phenomena of their own, but the moons and ring systems they possess are amazing environments awaiting further exploration. In this presentation, we'll explore these unique worlds and discuss the missions and discoveries to date. We'll continue outward to explore Pluto and the Kuiper Belt Objects that have been found.

ALL ABOUT CHOCOLATE
SUNDAY, FEBRUARY 4 AT 1:30 P.M.
Professional pastry chef Rose Deneen will explain the different types of chocolate as well as how to find and store good quality chocolate. She will demonstrate melting and making garnishes, candies and a quick chocolate mousse. Samples will be provided.
This program is sponsored by the Roselle Public Library Foundation.

ALEXIAN CONNECTS
IRRITABLE BOWEL SYNDROME—
NEW TREATMENT OPTIONS
MONDAY, FEBRUARY 12 AT 7:00 P.M.
Dr. Brian Muska, board certified gastroenterologist, will discuss how the embarrassing symptoms of IBS—abdominal pain, bloating, gas, diarrhea and constipation—could possibly represent something more serious. Twenty percent of American adults suffer from IBS but few seek treatment. The newest treatment options available and how best to control the symptoms will also be covered.
Registration required. Call AlexianConnects at 1-866-ALEXIAN (253-9426).

Adult Book Discussions

The first Adult Book Discussion of 2007 will be held on January 16, and will feature **In the Lake of the Woods** by Tim O'Brien. This is a novel about the Vietnam War, but only after it has ended. It affects a politician running for the U.S. Senate when it is revealed that he participated in a My Lai-type massacre while still a soldier.

 After losing the election in a landslide, his wife and he retreat to a cabin on a Minnesota lake, and his wife disappears. Was she murdered, or did she flee? Former lives and well-kept secrets are expertly revealed in this well-written novel. The author shows the reader how a war doesn't necessarily stop when a government decrees that it is over.

On February 20, the classic **Nineteen Eighty-Four**, by George Orwell, will be discussed. This is a horrific vision of totalitarian society. The main character, Winston Smith, works at the Ministry of Truth, where records, past and present, are 'corrected' so that they comply with the 'truth' that the Party wants to exist. In a grim city (London), where Big Brother is always watching and the Thought Police are always a threat, Winston is in grave danger because his memory is still functioning. This novel was once considered futuristic, but amazingly echoes the realities of contemporary times.

Around the Library...

Musical Sundays Winter Schedule

The Musical Sunday 2006-2007 season will run through May. We have several new performers, as well as some returning performers, this season.

December 17–**Kimberly Davis** will entertain us with classical piano music. She has been studying the piano since she was four years old, and has won numerous competitions. She is currently majoring in piano performance at the University of Illinois at Urbana-Champaign. After graduation, Kimberly plans on obtaining a Master's degree and possibly a PhD in piano performance.

January 21– **Sounds of Silver** will perform. This is a talented flute quartet that can play many different musical styles. They will perform primarily jazz, and will also provide an introduction to the flute for children. This promises to be fun for everyone.
This program is sponsored by the Roselle Public Library Foundation.

February 18–the harp will be played by **Marysue Redmann** for this Valentine's Day Musical Sunday. Marysue is a native of Chicago, and has studied and played the harp for nearly 25 years. She has played in major Chicago hotels, restaurants, and for numerous other events, including the inaugural ball of Mayor Richard M. Daley.

Musical Sundays are held in the atrium area of the library. No registration is required, and refreshments are served. All shows run from 1:30 until 3:00.

We hope you will join us for these unique and special shows.

The Midway Ramblers Cajun Band performed at the Library on September 17, 2006 to kick off the 2006/2007 Musical Sunday series.

Library offers service to homebound patrons

Library District residents who are homebound due to illness or disability may qualify to receive monthly library delivery service. Our outreach librarian would be happy to select books, audio or video materials for patrons based on their interests and drop them off on a regular schedule. If you or someone you know would like to receive this service, please call the Reference Department (630) 529-1641 ext. 211 for further information.

Subscribe to the Roselle Public Library Electronic News to get updated Library news and press releases delivered right to your computer!

http://www.roselle.lib.il.us/Newsletter/subscribe.html

Adult Computer Classes

INTERNET 101
JANUARY 18, 1:00—3:00 P.M.
FEBRUARY 22, 7:00 P.M.—9:00 P.M.
Learn how to navigate the Internet with confidence. Participants will get hands-on experience on the Library's Internet workstations. *Registration is required.*

INTRODUCTION TO E-MAIL
JANUARY 9, 10:00 A.M.—12:00 P.M.
FEBRUARY 5, 1:00—3:00 P.M.
Learn how to get an e-mail account, compose and send messages, and work with e-mail attachments. Participants, ages 12 and up, will get hands-on experience with the Library's Internet workstations. *Registration is required.*

COMPUTER BASICS CLASS
JANUARY 22, 7:00 P.M.—9:00 P.M.
FEBRUARY 10, 10:00 A.M. – 12:00 P.M.
The focus of this class will be on how to use the keyboard and mouse, creating word documents and creating and managing folders. Class size is limited to ensure plenty of one-on-one time with question and answer periods, and hands-on experience. *Registration is required.*

Youth Services

Holiday and
Special Programs

JUST FOR YOU!   ALL AGES
MONDAY, FEBRUARY 12   9:30 A.M. - 8:30 P.M.

A drop-in program featuring Valentine's Day crafts for children in the Youth Services department. An adult must accompany children 7 years-old and younger.

TEDDY BEAR TALES
SATURDAY, FEBRUARY 24   10:30-11:15 A.M.

Children ages 2-5 years old (siblings are welcome) with parents gather for stories, songs, and craft, and refreshments. Bring your own special teddy bear or stuffed animal friend.

(registration begins Monday, February 5)

FAMILY FLICKS

Drop-in to view a newly released family film. Dates, times and titles to be announced as information becomes available on movies to be released this winter. For the whole family, films shown are rated "G" or "PG". An adult must accompany children 7 years old and younger.

TEA WITH THE 2006 ROSE QUEEN
SATURDAY, MARCH 10   2:00 P.M.

Children in Kindergarten through 6th grade meet and spend time with the 2006 Rose Queen, Denise Hibbard. Each participant will design and make a tiara. Refreshments will be served.
A Roselle Library card is required to register for this program. Spaces are limited.

Saddle Up & Read, Bookaroo!

YOUTH SERVICES
WINTER READING PROGRAM
JANUARY 8 THROUGH MARCH 5, 2007

Read, or listen to, books and receive prizes for your reading this winter! Register for **Saddle Up & Read, Bookaroo!** to receive a game sheet to mark off minutes read, and a bookmark.

Check out materials from the Roselle Public Library to participate in the Youth Services Winter Reading Program 2007. Keep track of the number of minutes you read, or are read to, log in at the Youth Services "Ask Me" Desk and receive a prize at the 180-minute (3 hours) goal, the 360-minute (6 hours) goal, and the 540-minute (9 hours) goal. There will also be a grand prize drawing, with tickets given each time a participant logs in more minutes read during the Winter Reading Program 2007. For those wishing to continue reading past the 540-minute goal, bonus sheets will be available with a special bonus prize drawing.

Enjoy reading, and listening to, stories from the Youth Services' Fiction collections, follow the trail to interesting facts and learn new things from the Youth Services' Non-Fiction collection, listen to Audio Books on compact disc or cassette tapes – and earn incentive prizes by participating in **Saddle Up & Read, Bookaroo!** – **Youth Services Winter Reading Program 2007.** The final day to log in minutes read or receive prizes is Monday, March 5, 2007.

 Just click on the **TumbleBook Library** icon on the Youth Services page of the Roselle Public Library website and enter the world of **TumbleBooks**—e-books for kids.

Winter Storytime Schedule

Winter Session of Storytimes

begins registration Tuesday January 2nd. This will be a six-week session beginning Tuesday, January 16, and continuing through Thursday, February 22. *Child must be the required minimum age by the date the program session begins.*

Tots & Tykes	6–19 months	Tuesdays	1:00–1:30 p.m.	Registration Required
Toddler Tales	20–35 months	Tuesdays	10:00–10:30 a.m.	Registration Required
Preschool Storytime	3–5 Years	Wednesdays	10:00–10:30 a.m.	Registration Required
Preschool Storytime	3–5 Years	Wednesdays	1:00–1:30 p.m.	Registration Required
Family Drop-In	All Ages	Tuesdays	7:00–7:30 p.m.	No Registration
Morning Drop-In	Child / Parent	Thursdays	10:00–10:30 a.m.	No Registration

Youth Services

School Age and Holiday Programs

KREATIVE KIDS

Monthly programs for children **Kindergarten through Grade** 2 will feature both story sharing and facts on a different topic each month. Participants create a craft project based on the specific month's theme. Registration is required and space is limited.

"Santa's Helpers" 4:30-5:15 p.m.	Thursday, December 14 *(Registration begins Monday, November 27)*
"Howdy Partner" 4:30-5:15 p.m.	Thursday, January 18 *(Registration begins Tuesday January 2)*
"It's a Bear!" 4:30-5:15 p.m.	Thursday, February 15 *(Registration begins Monday, January 29)*

CHESS CLUB

The Roselle Public Library Youth Chess Club meets **Mondays, 4:00-5:00 p.m.** in the Library meeting room. Chess players **ages 7 – 17 years-old** work on expanding their strategies and skill levels while playing each other. The winter session begins on Monday, January 8 and continues through Monday, March 19.
Registration is ongoing.

"WHAT'S UP WITH KIDS!"

The Youth Services sponsored newsletter written by and for kids. Write original articles, poetry, book reviews, and stories. Submit original illustrations. See your work in print.
For children in grades 2-6.

Organizational Meeting	Monday, January 15 6:30-7:30 p.m.
Article Submission Meeting	Thursday, February 15 6:30-7:30 p.m.

ON THE TRAIL TO BOOK ADVENTURES
THURSDAY, JANUARY 25   4:30—5:30 P.M.

Children in grades 3 through 6 learn how to use the Library Catalog to find books, movies, music, and information sources for homework. Some of the newer books in the collection will be highlighted. Refreshments will be provided "along the trail."
Registration begins Monday, January 8

TALES TALL & SMALL
THURSDAY, FEBRUARY 22   4:30—5:15 P.M.

Children in grades 3 through 6 gather around a "winter campfire" for stories, songs, and treats. This event will be held INSIDE.
Registration begins Monday, February 5

CELEBRATE THE SEASON – WITH GUEST STORYTELLER LEANNE JOHNSON!
SATURDAY, NOVEMBER 25   1:00 P.M.

Families begin the 2006 Holiday Season by gathering in the Library Meeting Room for a presentation of seasonal stories and music with professional storyteller Leanne Johnson. Refreshments will be served. Following the program, Santa Claus visits to greet the children of Roselle. All ages are invited to attend.
(Tickets available beginning Monday, November 6)
This program is sponsored by the Roselle Public Library Foundation.

TRIMMING THE HOLIDAY TREE
MONDAY, NOVEMBER 27
9:30 A.M. - 8:30 P.M.

Drop-in to the Youth Services Storytime Room and create ornaments to trim the Youth Services Holiday Tree. For children of all ages. An adult must accompany children 7 years-old and younger.

WORLD BOOK ENCYCLOPEDIA ON-LINE

Starting a research project for school?
Looking for answers to a trivia game?
Access **World Book Encyclopedia On-Line** through the Roselle Public Library website from home or at the Library internet stations in Youth Services.
To use **World Book Encyclopedia On-Line** from home, users need to have a Roselle Public Library Card and a PIN (personal identification number).
To use this on-line database after 5:00 or on weekends in the Library, a Roselle Public Library Card is required.

DO YOU NEED HELP WITH HOMEWORK?
LIVE HOMEWORK HELP POWERED BY TUTOR.COM

Free homework help is available for students in 4th grade and up. On-line help for Math, Science, Language Arts, and Social Studies can be accessed through the Roselle Public Library website either at the Library or at home. The service is open to public use at the library on weekdays before 5:00 p.m. Those using this service at any time from home or after 5:00 p.m. at the Library need to have a Roselle Public Library card and PIN (personal identification number).

BLOGGER BOOK CLUB

An online book discussion for kids who love books for anyone who loves children's literature

http://www.roselle.lib.il.us/YouthServices/BookClub/BookClub.htm
Join us! We've been waiting for YOU!

Catch Up on Teen Corner

TEEN ADVISORY BOARD
WHEN: THURSDAY, NOVEMBER 16ᵀᴴ, 4-5 P.M.
WHO: 6ᵀᴴ GRADE AND UP

If you are a student in middle or high school, join our first monthly Teen Advisory Board in the Library Conference Room. Come and volunteer your ideas for programs, books, magazines, movies, the website, and the teen area. This is your chance to speak up for *your library!* Meet your new teen librarian, Lori, and share a snack! Please register by filling out an application found in the Teen Area. You will be contacted about when the next meeting will be held. Board size is limited.

TEEN FILM SOCIETY
WHEN: MONDAY, JANUARY 8ᵀᴴ, 6 TO 8:30 P.M.
WHO: 6ᵀᴴ GRADE THROUGH 12ᵀᴴ GRADE ONLY

Enjoy watching movies for free? We invite you to the Teen Film Society's first monthly meeting where you will catch *Edward Scissorhands* (PG-13) with Johnny Depp and Winona Ryder, share a snack, and vote on next months film.
Next Scheduled Meetings: 6 to 8:30 p.m. on February 5ᵗʰ and March 5ᵗʰ

TEENS GET ACTIVE
WHEN: WEDNESDAY, JANUARY 10ᵀᴴ, 4-5 P.M.
WHO: 7ᵀᴴ GRADE AND UP

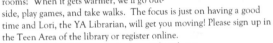

Want to get active outside of school sports? Join Teens Get Active (TGA). When the weather is cold, participate in low key aerobics to music in the meeting rooms! When it gets warmer, we'll go outside, play games, and take walks. The focus is just on having a good time and Lori, the YA Librarian, will get you moving! Please sign up in the Teen Area of the library or register online.

Scheduled Meetings in January: 17ᵗʰ, 24ᵗʰ, 31ˢᵗ
Scheduled Meetings in February: 7ᵗʰ, 14ᵗʰ, 21ˢᵗ, 28ᵗʰ
Scheduled Meetings in March: 7ᵗʰ, 14ᵗʰ, 21ˢᵗ, 28ᵗʰ

All meetings from 4-5 p.m. except Jan 24ᵗʰ and Mar 21ˢᵗ when we will start at 4:30 p.m.

TEEN WRITERS CLUB
WHEN: TUESDAY JANUARY 9ᵀᴴ, 6:30 TO 8 P.M.
WHO: 6ᵀᴴ GRADE AND UP

Do you like to write stories, comics, cartoons, poetry, or even news/magazine articles? Maybe you like to jot stuff down in a notebook but you want to put more time into it. Here's your chance! Join the Teen Writers Club and get support and feedback for your writing! We encourage you to bring anything that you're working on now or want to share from the past. If you're interested, we can start a Teen'zine! Please sign up in the Teen Area of the library or register online.
Next Scheduled Meetings: 6:30 to 8 p.m. on February 6ᵗʰ and March 6ᵗʰ

BABYSITTER TRAINING WORKSHOP
WHEN: SATURDAYS, JANUARY 27ᵀᴴ & FEBRUARY 3ᴿᴰ, 10:30 A.M. – 2:30 P.M.
WHO: STUDENTS AGES 10 - 16

Learn how to be a super babysitter! Register in person for the Babysitter Training Workshop beginning November 13ᵗʰ. The 2-day course will cover all aspects of babysitting. Each participant needs to bring a doll to practice on as well as a sack lunch and beverage to each session. A non-refundable $10.00 fee is due at registration. Class size is limited.

GOT HOMEWORK?

Get FREE help online from real tutors. One-to-one help.
Daily: 4:00 pm—10:00 pm

At home or at Roselle Public Library!
http://www.roselle.lib.il.us/AdultServices/Databases.htm

Math. Science. Social Studies. English.
GRADES 4–12 ◆ COLLEGE INTRO

Searching for Artistic Teen Talent

If you've got mad artistic skills, bring them here! Come see Lori, the YA Librarian, and she'll be happy to display your talent in the Teen Area of the library. Whether you draw anime, paint scenes, sketch portraits, sculpt creatures, or even work with crafts, Lori wants to exhibit your work for others to notice.

Hear! Hear!
Downloadable Audiobooks!

)) Digital audiobooks for all ages available at ListenIllinois

Downloadable AUDIOBOOKS!

)) Over 4,100 titles; 150+ new titles added every month

)) Download from anywhere to your PC; transfer to your MP3 player

For more information, browse to:
http://www.roselle.lib.il.us
Pull down the A-Z Quick Find Index
Click on "Downloadable Audiobooks"

FRIENDS
of the Roselle Public Library

The Friends of the Library had a successful Used Video Sale on October 7, 2006. They raised over $490 that they will use to support the Roselle Library over the coming months.

The day before the sale the Friends, all volunteers, worked hard organizing the Library Meeting Room for the sale. This included moving the Library AV withdrawals and the many AV donations the Library received from the community. On Saturday they had visitors of all ages and the Friends were very happy with the success of the sale.

Friends of the Library Membership Application

Name _____

Address _____

_____

Telephone _____

Email _____

Interests:

_____ Assist with Book Sales

_____ Plan Friends Fund-raisers

_____ Publicity

Other _____

Please return completed forms to the front desk at the Library, or mail to:

Roselle Public Library District
40 South Park Street
Roselle, IL 60172
Attention: Friends of the Library

Roselle Public Library
Foundation

The Roselle Public Library Foundation is looking for new members to help their Board develop fundraising projects. The Foundation uses these funds to build an endowment for the Library and some of the funds are donated to the Library annually to support special projects.

In the past these funds have been used to develop a classic and popular DVD collection, fund business newspaper journals and magazines, and finance programs. The Foundation is looking for members willing to volunteer their time and services to the Library.

The Roselle Library Foundation has funded a number of programs scheduled this winter. The Foundation has made it possible for the Library to expand the number of programs offered to the community. The Foundation has funded the following programs:

November 25, 2006 1:00 p.m.	*Celebrate the Season with Guest Storyteller Leanne Johnson*
January 21, 2007 1:30 p.m.	Musical Sunday *Sounds of Silver*
February 4, 2007 1:30 p.m.	*All About Chocolate*

Highlight your Hobby or Exhibit your Collection at the Library

The library's display case located on the first floor facing the Circulation Desk is available for exhibits by local hobbyists, collectors or non-profit organizations on a monthly basis. Patrons interested in displaying a collection can contact Debbie Miel at (630) 529-1641 ext. 211 (Reference Desk.)

AS A COURTESY TO OUR PATRONS...

Coffee is provided in the atrium Monday through Friday from 9:30 am to noon. Come and enjoy coffee and a book or magazine at the Library!

LIBRARY BOARD MEETINGS

Are the second Wednesday of every month at 7:30pm in the Library Conference Room.
The public is invited.

Help a Needy Family this Winter with our Mitten Tree

Come and decorate our "Mitten Tree" this December.
Please bring in NEW mittens, gloves and hats to the Circulation Department.
All items will be donated to the Bloomingdale Township General Assistance Office, which will distribute them to families in need within our community.

New Calendar! @ Your Library

 Roselle Public Library now offers a quick and easy way to look up and **sign-up** for library programs and events right from your home computer!

With the new online Calendar of Events, you can search for just the programs you're interested in...Children's programs, musical programs, book discussions...you decide which programs appear on the calendar! Display more information with one click.

Email the information to a friend, print it, download it to your calendar, and register all on the same screen. You can even opt to receive email notification of similar programs automatically! And the best part...do all this on your schedule, anytime, 24 hours a day/7 days a week.

Browse to the Library's website: http://www.roselle.lib.il.us
Pull down the A-Z Quick Find Index and click on "Calendar of Events" to get started.

ABINGTON COMMUNITY LIBRARY

FROM THE STACKS

Abington
Community
Library

FALL 2006

ACL Wins Statewide Marketing Award

Abington Community Library (ACL) recently won a marketing award from the Office of Commonwealth Libraries' Bureau of Library Development. The award, which is presented annually to only three libraries within the state, recognizes those libraries that excel in promoting their facilities as resources for lifelong learning. The ACL was honored for its marketing to the community.

"Lots of places offer education; we aim to offer free, educational resources and programming to patrons of all ages," said Leah Rudolph, MLIS, director of the ACL.

Bonnie Young, Public Library Advisor with the Office of Commonwealth Libraries' Bureau of Library Development, noted that it was the library's tagline and "The Ideal Patron" campaign that made the ACL stand out among other libraries vying for the award.

The tagline, "Committed to Lifelong Learning," was conceived by public relations staff person Tricia Richards. It was used along with the library's logo to create a sense of "corporate identity" within the community.

Cont., p. 3

FRIENDS OF THE ACL MAKES $10,000 DONATION TOWARD BOOK PURCHASES

Friends of the Abington Community Library, a volunteer organization which supports library programs and services, has made a $10,000 gift to the library for the purchase of new books.

"With such a generous gift, we'll be able to purchase both print and audio books to serve a number of purposes," said ACL Director Leah Ducato Rudolph. "We plan to expand our offerings for reference, adult, and children's books, plus audio books."

"The Friends board is pleased to make this donation to the library," stated Laura Santoski, president of the Friends of the ACL.

"We view the library as both an essential component of and a gift to the Abington community, and we're thrilled that we're able to help the library expand its collection."

Books purchased as a result of this donation will be marked with stickers to acknowledge the Friends of the ACL gift.

Funds were raised from used book sales which the group conducts on a semi-annual basis. With all public sales, books, music and movies in good condition are donated and sold to benefit the library.

Friends of the Abington Community Library has donated $10,000 for the purchase of books. Shown at the check presentation are, from left: Laura Santoski, Friends president; Jim Kalp, Friends board member/book sale volunteer; Ronnie Dende, Friends board member/book sale co-chairperson; and Leah Ducato Rudolph, library director. Absent from photo is Beth Florey, Friends board member and book sale co-chairperson.

The last two sales each generated about $5,000 in revenue, which the Friends of the ACL board has voted to earmark for books.

"I would be remiss if I didn't thank the community for its generous donations to and support of our used book sales," Santoski added.

"Without the volume and quality of the books and media we received, we would not have been able to raise the funds necessary to provide such a donation to the library. It's truly a collaborative effort between the people of the Abingtons and Friends of the library."

The next used book sale is

slated for Saturday, Oct. 14, 2006, at the Clarks Summit United Methodist Church. Preview night is October 13 for Friends members.

The Friends of the ACL conducts other special events throughout the year, with some programs free or discounted for members.

To join, complete and return the membership form on page 6.

The next Friends of the ACL used book sale will be October 14. For more information, see page 6.

Summer Reading Stats

More than 250 children received certificates for completing the requirements of the Children's Summer Reading Program this year. At the ACL, the 425 children registered read a total of 5,344 books! The Children's Summer Reading Program ran June 12 through August 4.

Seventy-seven participants in the Teen Read Program (grades 7-12) read a record number of books: 682! The most books read by one teen was 36.

Thanks to those who donated their time to make this event a success: Lackawanna County; The Abington Heights Civic League; Narda Tafuri & Northeast Dogs; Ann Whitney of Rainbow's End Greyhound Rescue; Al Ondush, Pat McClane, Cheryl O'Hora, and Alexsandra Djordjevic.

OFFICERS ANNOUNCED FOR LIBRARY BOARD

The Abington Community Library Board of Directors met recently to elect officers. Board officers are, front row from left: Mary Jo Kelly, treasurer; Richard Fanning, president; Bernard Harding, immediate past president; Margaret Kelly, vice president; and Rebecca Roberts, secretary. Additional board members, shown in back row from left, are: Jean Marie Decker, Hong Nguyen, Robin Domenico, Charles Dougherty, Barry Kaplan, Edward Klovensky, Elvin LaCoe, Karen Brier, Janet McCabe, Timothy Habeeb, Adrienne Horger and Abington Community Library Director Leah Ducato Rudolph. Absent from photo are board members Clara Adcroft, C. Martin Kelly, and Constance Sheils.

September is National Library Card Sign-Up Month ~ Treat Yourself to a Library Card!

September is National Library Card Sign-Up Month! To celebrate the event, we're treating our card holders to a sweet surprise at the Abington Community Library. Sign up for your free card today, re-activate an expired one, or replace a lost card. All patrons who check out material during the month will have the opportunity to enter a free drawing for treats.

Remember that children and teens need their own library cards to use computers— give them a "taste" of independence by getting a card for each child today.

Savor the benefits of a Lackawanna County Library System card:
- Free loan of books, talking books, movies and music
- Access to free Internet services—we even offer wireless connection, courtesy of Adelphia Communications
- Free educational and recreational programs and events
- Freedom to go online from any computer to search the catalog, place holds, renew materials, read library newsletters, and more!
- Use of reference materials and reference services
- Access to more than 40 databases
- Admission to special events—and more!

*"New" refers to applications for new cards, renewed cards (cards expire after three years with no use), or replacement cards.
Hershey's, Mr. Goodbar and Krackel are registered trademarks of Hershey Foods, Inc.

new*
Get your free library card and use it today!
It's a sweet deal!
All card holders may enter a drawing for other sweet treats!

The tagline and logo were included in all print and electronic communications.

The Ideal Patron campaign comprised a series of posters depicting individuals of various ages using the library's resources for specific needs.

In order to keep costs down, posters initially were created with stock photos, Richards said. Later, local photographer Guy Cali volunteered to provide custom digital images, so the library was able to recreate the posters using photos of actual patrons.

"We are a community library, so it made sense to involve the community in creating The Ideal Patron campaign," said Richards. "Staff member Gisela Butera planted the seed of telling the public about the library's collections, services and technological resources, and the idea grew from there," she added.

Shown with the award are, from left: Tricia Richards, ACL public relations representative; Pamela Murphy, district consultant for the Lackawanna County Library System; Richard Fanning, president, ACL board of directors; and Leah Ducato Rudolph, ACL director.

"Leah and Tricia worked very hard and can be a model to libraries of all sizes across the state. I just loved the slogan, "Committed to Lifelong Learning," all the promotions…and the heartwarming and meaningful posters that demonstrate what a public library truly is," said Young.

"We are especially pleased to have won, since the judges gave us credit not only for concept development and marketing skill, but also for the fiscal responsibility we demonstrated with execution of our ideas," said Richards.

As a representative of a winning library, Rudolph will be part of a panel discussion about these concepts at the PA Library Convention in Pittsburgh this November. She is "quite excited to share our philosophy of consistent, professional publicity, fiscally responsible marketing, teamwork and commitment to lifelong learning with other libraries in the Commonwealth."

Thanks to All of Our Ideal Patrons!

While *all* of its patrons are ideal, the Abington Community Library staff is especially grateful to those who participated in our Ideal Patron campaign (details above). Images like the one below appear on the posters, with captions to indicate that those pictured use the library resources for specific business or personal needs. Examples of the captions are included below:

"Uses the 40+ databases through PA Power Library for business purposes" (mom)
"Enjoys game night at the library" (girl)
"Uses online services to place holds and renew materials" (boy)

"Are members of Friends of the Abington Community Library" (family)
"Attends programs at the library together" (family)

Visit the Abington Community Library to view the entire collection. It will be completed and hung in the library soon.

Canned Goods Drive in November; Conducted by ACL Teen Literature Committee

You'll be asked to bring more than just your library card and a thirst for information when you visit the Abington Community Library this November.

The library's Teen Literature Committee is sponsoring "Kit's Thanks-giving Canned Goods Drive" for the entire month. The drive will directly benefit Safety Net, a non-profit agency located in Scranton that helps people other agencies cannot. Infant and supplemental food, rent, prescriptions, eyeglasses, furniture and moving assistance are provided to people who "fell through the cracks."

Event Chairperson Hayley Lenahan explained the rationale behind the program: "Our community has been so good to the library, and we'd like to return the favor by passing along something meaningful at a time of year when it's most appreciated."

Non-perishable goods may be dropped off in specially marked boxes near the library's Circulation Desk. Recommended items include: canned fruit or vegetables, boxed stuffing, soup, cereal, pasta, baby food, formula and diapers.

The month-long collection will end on December 1 with a program revolving around Kit, an American Girl doll whose story takes place during the Depression.

Thanks in advance to everyone who contributes so that others may give thanks.

FALL PROGRAMS FOR ALL AGES

PROGRAM NOTES: Most programs will be conducted in the Ryon Room, unless otherwise noted. All computer classes will take place in the Media Room, near the Reference Desk. Please register for programs by visiting the library or calling (570) 587-3440. For more information on these and other programs, visit the Abington Community Library website, www.lclshome.org/Abington and click on "Library Events."

DATE	TIME	PROGRAM	AGES
SEPTEMBER EVENTS			
Sept 11-Oct 9	Multiple	Story Time for Ages 2 & 3, Mondays and Wednesdays at 10:30 AM	Ages 2 & 3
Sept 11-Oct 9	Multiple	Story Time for Ages 3—5, Tuesdays at 10:30 AM and 1:30 PM	Ages 3—5
Tues., Sept. 12	10 AM—Noon	Laptop Quilting with RSVP Volunteer Peg Winter / WAIT LIST ONLY	Adults
Sept. 15-Nov. 17	10:30 AM	1-2-3 Story and Playtime / alternate Fridays for total of six sessions	Ages 12-36 months
Fri., Sept. 15	11 AM	Car Seat Laws, Appropriate Seats, & Safety Tips with PA State Trooper Connie Devens	All ages
Sat., Sept. 16	10 AM—Noon	Friends of the ACL Café (see article, p. 6)	All ages
Sat., Sept. 16	11 AM	Coming to Your Senses: An Introduction to Sign Language with Lori Conniff, Scranton State School for the Deaf	Grades 4-6
Tues., Sept. 19	10 AM—Noon	Laptop Quilting with RSVP Volunteer Peg Winter / WAIT LIST ONLY	Adults
Tues., Sept. 19	7 PM	Dybbuk Book discussion	Adults
Wed., Sept. 20	3 PM	Don't Let's Go to the Dogs Tonight Afternoon Book Discussion	Adults
Thurs., Sept. 21	7-7:45 PM	Celebrate Johnny Appleseed's Birthday: Apple stories, crafts.	Ages 4-8
Thurs., Sept. 21	7 PM	Hear Author David McCullough at the Scranton Cultural Center	All ages
Sat., Sept. 23	10-11 AM	Microsoft Word® (Basic) with Marywood University Volunteer Instructors	Adults
Thurs., Sept. 28	3-4 PM	Teacher Appreciation Open House	Teachers by invitation
Fri., Sept. 29	3:30-5:30 PM	Make-It, Take-It Crafts: Fall Is Here! (drop in anytime during program)	Ages 3-12
OCTOBER EVENTS			
All month		Pumpkins on Parade (see article, p. 6)	All ages
Tues., Oct. 3	10 AM—Noon	Laptop Quilting with RSVP Volunteer Peg Winter / WAIT LIST ONLY	Adults
Tues., Oct. 3	6:30-8 PM	Breathe Easier: Answers to Sinus Problems with Dr. Seth Linker	Adults
Wed., Oct. 4	7 PM	Bipolar Disorders with Dr. A.C. Patel	Adults
Thurs., Oct. 5	7 PM	Fire Prevention & Safety with Dan Police	All ages
Sat., Oct. 7	Multiple	Fire Engine Story Time and Craft / Sponsored by the ACL-TLC Choose one of three sessions: 10-10:30 AM; 10:30-11 AM; 11-11:30 AM	Up to 10 years
Mon., Oct. 9	**CLOSED FOR COLUMBUS DAY HOLIDAY**		
Tues., Oct. 10	10 AM-Noon	Laptop Quilting with RSVP Volunteer Peg Winter / WAIT LIST ONLY	Adults
Sat., Oct. 14	9 AM-2 PM	Friends of the ACL Used Book Sale and Café (see article, p. 6)	All ages

DATE	TIME	PROGRAM	AGES
OCTOBER EVENTS, cont.			
Oct. 15-Oct. 21		Teen Read Week: Get Active @ Your Library	Teens
Sun., Oct. 15	TBA	LCLS Battle of the Bands. Contact your local library for details.	All ages
Tues., Oct. 17	10 AM-Noon	Laptop Quilting with RSVP Volunteer Peg Winter / WAIT LIST ONLY	Adults
Tues., Oct. 17	7 PM	Metamorphosis Book Discussion	Adults
Fri., Oct. 20	4-? PM	Chess Tournament	Grades 7-12
Sat., Oct. 21	10 AM-Noon	Friends of the ACL Café (see article, p. 6)	All ages
Sat., Oct. 21	10-11 AM	Google® Searching Class with Marywood University Volunteer Instructors	Adults
Mon., Oct. 23	3:30-5:30 PM	Halloween Crafts (drop in anytime during program)	Ages 3-12
Tues., Oct. 24	10 AM-Noon	Laptop Quilting with RSVP Volunteer Peg Winter / WAIT LIST ONLY	Adults
Tues., Oct. 24	7 PM	More Genealogy Research with Kate Gibbons	Adults
Oct. 30-Nov. 29	Multiple	Story Time for Ages 2 & 3, Mondays and Wednesdays at 10:30 AM	Ages 2 & 3
Oct. 30-Nov. 29	Multiple	Story Time for Ages 3—5, Tuesdays at 10:30 AM and 1:30 PM	Ages 3-5
TBA	TBA	Scary Stories for Grades 4-6—Check library for date and time.	Grades 4-6
Tues., Oct. 31	10 AM-Noon	Laptop Quilting with RSVP Volunteer Peg Winter / WAIT LIST ONLY	Adults
Tues., Oct. 31	6-8 PM	Horror Movies Starring Boris Karloff	Teens
NOVEMBER EVENTS			
All month		Kit's Thanks-giving Canned Goods Collection (see article, p. 3)	All ages
Sat., Nov. 4	10-11 AM	Microsoft Word® (Part 2)	Adults
Sun., Nov. 5	2 PM	Children's Author Margie Palatini at the Scranton Cultural Center	All ages
Tues., Nov. 7	**CLOSED FOR ELECTION DAY**		
Thurs., Nov. 9	7 PM	A Veteran Remembers … with Abe Plotkin	Grade 7-Adult
Sat., Nov. 11	**CLOSED FOR VETERANS DAY**		
Nov. 13-19		Children's Book Week (Contests TBA)	
Mon., Nov. 13	10:30 AM-Noon	Answers to Children's Ear, Nose & Throat Problems with Dr. Seth Linker	Adults
Tues., Nov. 14	10 AM-Noon	Laptop Quilting with RSVP Volunteer Peg Winter / WAIT LIST ONLY	Adults
Thurs., Nov. 16	7 PM	America Around the Time of the Pilgrims (in Hand-carved Wood) with	Grades 7-Adult
Fri., Nov. 17	7-8 PM	Gingerbread Houses / Children's Room	All ages
Sat., Nov. 18	10 AM-Noon	Friends of the ACL Café (see article, p. 6)	All ages
Sat., Nov. 18	10 AM-Noon	Gingerbread Houses / Children's Room	All ages
Tues., Nov. 21	7 PM	Puttermesser Papers Book Discussion	Adults
Wed., Nov. 22	5 PM	Early Closing for Thanksgiving Holiday	
Thurs., Nov. 23	**CLOSED FOR THANKSGIVING HOLIDAY**		

USED BOOK SALE OCTOBER 14

Friends of the Abington Community Library will sponsor a used book sale and café on Saturday, Oct. 14, from 9 AM to 2 PM at the Clarks Summit United Methodist Church, located at the corner of West Grove Street and the Morgan Highway.

Sponsored by the ACL Teen Literature Committee, the café will be open until noon and will feature coffee, tea, bottled water and baked goods.

In addition, volunteers will be on hand to accept financial donations to cover the cost of shipping some unsold paperback books to active military from our area.

Friends members may attend the preview night on Friday, Oct. 13, at 5 PM. Attendees must be members in good standing and <u>must</u> assist with set-up prior to making selections/purchases.

Donations of materials in good condition are being accepted at the library during regular business hours through Sept. 23. Acceptable materials include hardcover and paperback fiction and non-fiction for adults and young adults, children's books, DVDs, VHS tapes, audio books, and computer software.

Volunteers are needed for clean-up at the conclusion of the book sale. Call 587-3440 for details.

Join Friends of the ACL today and use the valuable coupon in this newsletter!

Pumpkins on Parade This October
Patrons Invited to Decorate for Season

Beginning October 2, you can register to be eligible for a free pumpkin to be carved, painted or decorated at home, then returned to the library for everyone to enjoy.

Pumpkins will be issued on a first-come, first-served basis during the week of October 23. They must be returned to the Abington Community Library by October 29, where they will remain on display until November 4.

Signs will be put in front of each completed pumpkin to identify the person(s) who did them.

Whether or not you decorate a pumpkin for the library's seasonal décor, please come to enjoy them as we celebrate autumn!

Friends Café Offers Socialization, Relaxation ... and Did We Mention Free Coffee, Tea and Baked Goods?

Friends of the ACL is pleased to announce the opening of its café this fall! Conducted once a month for three months, this is a pilot program to determine if library patrons have interest in enjoying a hot cup of coffee while reading their newspapers and library books or sipping tea while listening to the new CD releases at the library.

Hosted by Friends of the ACL board members, the Café is designed to not only provide a comfortable place to read and chat, but also to allow people to explore library services at their leisure. Mark your calendars for September 16, October 21 and November 18! Café hours are 10 a.m. to Noon each of those days.

Wal-Mart recently made a financial donation to the Abington Community Library to help make improvements to the library's young adult area. Shown at the check presentation are, from left: Gisela Butera, library staff member; Hayley Lenahan, teen literature committee representative; and Nora Minnick, Wal-Mart community relations representative.

Teen Literature Committee Welcomes New Members

If you're in grades 7 through 12 and you'd like to be part of an exciting peer group which benefits the Abington Community Library, please let us know!

You'll meet other students who share your interests ... you'll be able to create, plan and execute various public programs ... you'll develop project management and leadership skills ... and you'll develop fantastic contacts to help you with future goals.

Learn more about the teen board at the Abington Community Library by calling Mrs. Leah Ducato Rudolph, TLC adviser, at (570) 587-3440.

FRIEND TO FRIEND

For members of Friends of the Abington Community Library

MESSAGE FROM THE PRESIDENT

As fall approaches, the Board of Directors of the Friends of the Abington Community Library is ready to embark on a new year of enjoyable and informative events and programs. Before noting those, I'll update you on events since the last newsletter.

Officers, New Members Announced

At its spring meeting, the Board elected new officers and added four new members to its ranks. Officers for the 2006-2007 year are: Laura Santoski, president; Jim Kalp and Tricia Richards, vice presidents; Ceil Bowen, treasurer; and Tricia Richards, secretary. The new board members are: Heidi Caminiti, Carol Harrison, Cathie Hartman and Peggy Lyons.

Book Sales

The June book sale was a tremendous success. Thanks to the community's generous donations, the Friends took in close to $5,000. And thanks to the volunteers who gave their time and muscle to setting up, taking down and working at the sale; we couldn't have done it without you!

The mini book sale in July also went well, with revenues of slightly more than $1,000.

Fall Café Scheduled

As I mentioned earlier, fall programming is off to a great start. Beginning Sept. 16, the Friends will sponsor a Saturday morning café in the Ryon Room at the library. The café will be offered the third Saturday in September, October and November from 10 am to noon. We hope you'll take advantage of the opportunity to sit down, sip some coffee or tea, and relax with a newspaper, magazine or checked-out book. It's a great way to start off your Saturday!

Important Membership Changes

On a final note, I'd like to advise you of a change in

Four women have been appointed to the board of directors of the Friends of the ACL. Shown in the front row, from left, are Carol Harrison and Heidi Caminiti. Back row, from left, are Cathie Hartman and Peggy Lyons.

Friends' membership. Beginning in January, our fiscal year will be based on the calendar year. ***Accordingly, all current Friends' memberships will expire in December of this year. Memberships must be renewed early next year in order to remain active.***

We are sorry for any confusion or inconvenience this may cause, but the change is essential for more effective bookkeeping and membership tracking.

Membership dues will change beginning in January. Individual dues will remain at $5 per year; family dues will increase to $10 per year.

As always, the Board welcomes your input and your willingness to participate in its endeavors. If you'd like to contribute an idea or to volunteer, please let us know by dropping us a note at the library. We look forward to hearing from you!

Warm regards,
Laura Santoski
President, *Friends of the ACL*

WE'D LOVE TO HAVE MORE *FRIENDS!*

Enjoy membership in *Friends of the Abington Community Library!* For just $5, you'll be invited to *Friends*-only events, take advantage of discounts to selected programs, and get a sneak peek at our used book sales the night before they are open to the public!*

Simply complete this membership form and leave it at the Circulation Desk with your $5 check or mail it to the library. All proceeds benefit the Abington Community Library.

*Must assist with set-up prior to making selections/purchases.

YES! I want to join/renew my membership! Enclosed is my check for $5, made payable to *Friends of the ACL. Membership expires Dec. 31, 2006.*

NAME _____

ADDRESS _____

_____

E-MAIL _____

Please leave this at the library Circulation Desk or mail to: Friends of the Abington Community Library, 1200 W. Grove St., Clarks Summit, PA 18411. Thank you!

FRIENDS-ONLY BOOK SALE COUPON

This coupon is valid for one item with a book sale value of up to $2. Coupon must be surrendered when redeemed. Photocopies not accepted. One coupon per person. Coupon may not be exchanged for cash.

Coupon valid for Oct. 14, 2006 book sale only.

1200 W. Grove St.
Clarks Summit, PA 18411

Phone: (570) 587-3440
E-mail: abiadmin@albright.org

www.lclshome.org/Abington

For upcoming programs, click
on "Library Events."

Ask a reference librarian for
information about Power
Library, a collection of reliable
databases for professional and
personal reference.

Regular Library Hours
Mon-Fri   *9 am – 9 pm*
Sat   *9 am – 5 pm*
Sun   *2 pm – 5 pm*

Ask Here PA Debuts September 6; 24-Hour Online Library Reference Service for Pennsylvanians

In early August, Governor Edward G. Rendell announced that a new virtual chat service will debut September 6 to help people get information from a library.

"Ask Here PA," a first for Pennsylvania, will be available to everyone in Pennsylvania 24 hours a day, seven days a week. The service begins September 6.

Albright Memorial Library, Scranton, is one of 90 public and academic libraries from across the commonwealth which will participate. Libraries are voluntarily contributing staff to help "Ask Here PA" become a useful, successful tool.

Students and the public will be able to reach public librarians, while college students and faculty will be helped by librarians from participating colleges and universities. Staff from the participating libraries will provide reference assistance to patrons during the day. An international cooperative of libraries will cover the overnight hours.

Eleven libraries are currently testing the program and training librarians to help online users. From noon to 5 p.m., inquirers may use the "Ask Here PA" homepage or access library Web sites through Villanova University, Free Library of Philadelphia, State Library of Pennsylvania, Scranton Public Library, James V. Brown Library/North Central Library District, Cambria County Library, Carnegie Library of Pittsburgh, Bethlehem Area Public Library, Kutztown University, DeSales University, and Bloomsburg University.

People may access the service through the Web site of all participating public libraries (Albright Memorial Library, www.lclshome.org/Albright) or through the home page at www.askherepa.org.

The Abington Community Library is a wireless hot spot, courtesy of Adelphia Communications. Bring your laptop and log on to the library website, www.lclshome.org/Abington to access your account, hold or renew materials, check upcoming activities, and access more than 40 databases through PA POWER Library.

Abington Community Library
Committed to lifelong learning.

Appendix H

Marketing Bibliography

Prepared by Bonnie McCloskey

Chapter 1

Barber, Peggy, and Linda Wallace. *What's the Message? Is Anyone Listening? A Communications Audit Can Help You Find Out.* Available at http://www.ssdesign.com/librarypr/content/p030402a.shtml (accessed May 29, 2007).

Choo, Chun Wei. *Information Management for the Intelligent Organization: The Art of Scanning the Environment.* Medford, NJ: Information Today, 2002.

Cooper, Sandra M., Nancy Bolt, Keith Curry Lance, and Lawrence Webster. *Community Analysis Methods and Evaluative Options: The CAMEO Handbook.* Available at http://skyways.lib.ks.us/pathway/cameo/ (accessed June 4, 2007).

DeRosa, Cathy, Joanne Cantrell, Diane Cellentani, and Janet Hawk, et al. *Perceptions of Libraries and Information Resources: A Report to the OCLC Membership.* Dublin, OH: OCLC, 2005.

Eberhart, George M. *The Whole Library Handbook 4.* Chicago: American Library Association, 2006.

Higa-Moore, M. L., B. Bunnett, H. G. May, and C. A. Olney. "Use of Focus Groups in a Library's Strategic Planning Process." *Journal of the Medical Library Association* 90, no. 1 (2002): 86–92.

Koontz, Christie. "Stores and Libraries: Both Serve Customers!" *Marketing Library Services* 16, no. 1 (January/February 2002). Available at http://www.infotoday.com/mls/jan02/koontz.htm (accessed May 29, 2007).

Leonhardt, Thomas W. "Taking Issue with OCLC's Environmental Scan." *Technicalities* 24, no. 6 (November/December 2004): 3–5.

McNamara, Carter. *Strategic Planning (In Nonprofit or For-Profit Organizations).* Available at http://www.managementhelp.org/plan_dec/str_plan/str_plan.htm#anchor320862 (accessed May 29, 2007).

Noack, Jennyann, ed. *Marketing the Library.* Columbus: Ohio Library Foundation, 2003. Available at http://www.olc.org/marketing/ (accessed May 29, 2007).

Weingand, Darlene E. *Marketing / Planning Library and Information Services.* 2nd ed. Englewood, CO: Libraries Unlimited, 1999.

Westbrook, Lynn. "Analyzing Community Needs: A Holistic Approach." *Library Administration & Management* 14, no. 1 (2000): 26–30.

Chapter 2

Center for Rural Studies. *Guidelines for Using the Nominal Group Technique.* Available at http://crs.uvm.edu/gopher/nerl/group/a/meet/Exercise7/b.html (accessed May 29, 2007).

Fisher, Patricia H., and Marseille M. Pride. *Blueprint for Your Library Marketing Plan: A Guide to Help You Survive and Thrive.* Chicago: American Library Association, 2005.

Hart, Keith. *Putting Marketing Ideas into Action.* London: Library Association Publishing, 1999.

Kassel, Amelia. "Marketing: Realistic Tips for Planning and Implementation in Special Libraries." *Information Outlook* 6, no.11 (November 2002): 6–8, 10.

Owens, Irene. *Strategic Marketing in Library and Information Science.* Binghamton, NY: Haworth Information Press, 2003.

Sample, John A. "Nominal Group Technique: An Alternative to Brainstorming." *Journal of Extension* 22, no. 2 (March 1984). Available at http://www.joe.org/joe/1984march/iw2.html (accessed May 29, 2007).

Stover, J. *Library Marketing: Thinking Outside the Book.* Available at http://librarymarketing.blogspot.com/ (accessed May 29, 2007).

University of Oregon, Academic Learning Services. *Leading a Discussion Using the Nominal Group Technique.* Available at http://tep.uoregon.edu/services/newsletter/year95-96/issue30/nominal.html (accessed May 29, 2007).

University of Wisconsin—Extension. *Quick Tips: Collecting Group Data: Nominal Group Technique.* Available at http://www.uwex.edu/ces/pdande/resources/pdf/Tipsheet3.pdf (accessed May 29, 2007).

Walters, Suzanne. *Library Marketing That Works!* New York: Neal-Schuman, 2004.

Weingand, Darlene E. *Marketing/Planning Library and Information Services.* 2nd ed. Englewood, CO: Libraries Unlimited, 1999.

Woodward, Jeannette. *Creating the Customer-Driven Library: Building on the Bookstore Model.* Chicago: American Library Association, 2004.

Chapter 3

American Library Association. *A Communications Handbook for Libraries.* Available at www.ala.org/ala/pio/availablepiomat/online_comm_handbook.pdf (accessed May 29, 2007).

American Library Association. *Media Relations Tools.* Available at http://www.ala.org/ala/pio/mediarelationsa/mediarelations/Default2270.htm (accessed May 29, 2007).

Block, M. "The Secret of Library Marketing: Make Yourself Indispensable." *American Libraries* 32, no. 8 (September 2001): 48–50

Dobi, Tia. "Press, Profit, and Provocation: Library Promotion for the Over-Educated." *Ex Libris: E-Zine for Librarians and Information Junkies.* Available at http://marylaine.com/exlibris/xlib229.html (accessed May 29, 2007).

Karp, Rashelle S., ed. *Powerful Public Relations: A How-to Guide for Libraries.* Chicago: American Library Association, 2002.

Kessler, Jane, and Carol Anne Germain. "Extra! Extra! Extra! Read All About It! Fundamentals of Good Press Releases." *Public Libraries* no. 5 (September/October 2003): 300–302.

O'Keefe, Claudia. "Publicity 101." *American Libraries* 36, no. 6 (June/July 2005): 52–55.

Parkhurst, William. *How to Get Publicity and Make the Most of It Once You Do*. New York: HarperCollins, 2000.

"Public Service Announcements." *Library Imagination Paper* 25, no. 4 (Fall 2003):1-1.

Reed, Sally Gardner. *Making the Case for Your Library*. New York: Neal-Shuman, 2001.

Siess, Judith A. *The Visible Librarian: Asserting Your Value with Marketing and Advocacy*. Chicago: American Library Association, 2003.

Stuhlman, D. "Think Like a Business, Act Like a Library: Library Public Relations." *Information Outlook* 7, no. 9 (September 2003): 10–13.

Texas Library Association. *PR Rx Toolkit*. Available at http://www.txla. org/html/toolkit/ (accessed May 29, 2007).

Wolfe, Lisa A. *Library Public Relations, Promotions, and Communications*. New York: Neal-Schuman, 2005.

Chapter 4

Bancel, Marilyn, and the Fund Raising School. *Preparing Your Capital Campaign*. San Francisco: Jossey-Bass, 2000.

Bennett, Linda. "Creating Partnerships That Pay Off." *The Bottom Line: Managing Library Finances* 18, no. 2 (2005): 92–94.

Bray, Ilona M. *Effective Fundraising for Nonprofits: Real World Strategies That Work*. Berkeley, CA: NOLO, 2005.

Herring, Mark Y. *Raising Funds with Friends Groups*. New York: Neal-Schuman, 2004.

Reed, Sally Gardner, Beth Nawalinski, and Alex Peterson. *101+ Great Marketing and Fundraising Ideas for Libraries and Friends*. New York: Neal-Schuman, 2004.

Sanderbeck, A., and P. Chiarmonte. *Proven Streams of Revenue for Under Funded Libraries*. Available at http://www.dynix.com/institute/archive. asp (accessed May 29, 2007).

Steele, Victoria, and Stephen D. Elder. *Becoming a Fundraiser: The Principles and Practice of Library Development.* Chicago: American Library Association, 2000.

Swan, James. *Fundraising for Libraries: 25 Proven Ways to Get More Money for Your Library.* New York: Neal-Schuman, 2002.

Taft Group for American Library Association. *The Big Book of Library Grant Money 2006: Profiles of Private and Corporate Foundations and Direct Corporate Givers Receptive to Library Grant Proposals.* Chicago: American Library Association, 2005.

Index

About the Author

SUSAN WEBRECK ALMAN has been interested in interpersonal communication for librarians (library marketing, PR, and advocacy) for two decades. She teaches communication courses to graduate students in library and information science on a regular basis. Her students are enthusiastic about her expertise and teaching style. She received degrees (MLS and PhD) from the University of Pittsburgh. Her career has included public service and administrative posts in libraries and teaching at the University of Michigan. Currently she is the Director of Distance Education Services and Outreach at the University of Pittsburgh and adjunct faculty at San Jose State University.